ESSENTIALS OF MONITORING AND EVALUATION – A HANDBOOK FOR ADMINISTRATORS AND MANAGERS

By, 'Yemi Adeyemi-Enilari

'Yemi Adeyemi-Enilari

DEDICATION

This book is dedicated to all those trying to make our lives, communities, and the world a better place to live in through the scientific and perhaps sometimes unintended and unknowing use of the principles of Monitoring and Evaluation.

Table of Contents

INTRODUCTION

Monitoring and Evaluation ideas are not new – everyone applies Monitoring and Evaluation practices and principles to some extent in their personal, work and home lives, even in many of our domestic chores like cooking, people are unknowingly applying the principles of Monitoring and Evaluation.

However, we are currently witnessing an increase in the amount of systematic attention and study being applied to the field of Monitoring and Evaluation (M&E) everywhere.

This is a very interesting and exciting development, as the practice of Monitoring & Evaluation can contribute to sound governance in and within an organisation and the society (community and nation) in several ways: improved evidence-based policy making, including, but not limited to budgeting and decision making, policy development, management, and accountability.

Many governments around the world have realised much of this potential, including most first-world countries, and a small but growing number of developing countries.

The objectives of this handbook are threefold:

✓ Firstly, basic Monitoring and Evaluation terms and concepts will be explained and discussed. This is to help you apply these terms to your work, and generally to other spheres of endeavour.

✓ Secondly, this handbook will provide you with the knowledge and skills that you can use in managing interventions within whatever sector you operate or may want to operate in.

✓ Finally, this handbook will relate generic Monitoring and Evaluation concepts to some known/familiar sectors specifically.

As a consultant to Nigerian government parastatals (local, state, and federal), as well as to some International Organisations, including some United Nations Agencies, World Bank, and USAID-sponsored projects and programmes on various aspects and sectors, examples will be drawn from those experiences.

ABOUT THIS HANDBOOK

Because it is a handbook, it is expected that readers are already familiar and conversant with Monitoring and Evaluation practices and principles, and probably are already using it on and for various projects and programmes. This handbook is designed and written for the reader/user to easily pick out key and necessary points in each chapter or/and point using 'bullet-points' for ease of reading in order to quickly see salient, relevant and necessary points in each chapter and section, rather than having to read through a lot of text.

So, in most (if not all) of the chapters, and with most points, bullet points are used with some short and brief explanations and introductions where it would be considered most necessary.

About "Programme and Project", for this handbook, both "project" and "programme" will be used interchangeably. But in chapter two (2), I will give the distinction (differences) and similarities between the two concepts.

CHAPTER ONE (1) – BASIC CONCEPTS AND DEFINITIONS

There are two (2) words in this concept/field of 'Monitoring and Evaluation,' these are "Monitoring" and "Evaluation", and to understand the field, the tool of study, I will give definitions and explanations, as well as explain the concepts of these two (2) words.

What Is Monitoring? The following are some of the most commonly used and accepted definitions of monitoring:

> ➢ Monitoring is the regular and continuous scientific observation and recording of activities taking place in a project or programme.
> ➢ It is a process of routinely gathering information on all aspects of the project.
> ➢ To monitor is to check on how project activities are progressing. It is a systematic and purposeful observation.
> ➢ Monitoring also involves giving feedback about the progress of the project to the donors/sponsors, implementers, and beneficiaries of the project.

Monitoring is a continuous process of collecting and analysing information about a programme and comparing actual against planned results to judge how well the intervention is being implemented. It uses the data generated by the programme itself (characteristics of individual participants, enrolment and attendance, end-of-programme situation of beneficiaries, and costs of the programme), and it makes for comparisons across individuals, types of programmes, and geographical locations. The existence of a reliable monitoring system is essential for evaluation.

Reporting enables the gathered information to be used in making decisions for improving project performance. Hence, knowing and understanding project objectives is of the essence, because how do you monitor what you do not know, even if it is right in front of you?

Steps To Monitoring: The following are steps necessary for effective monitoring:

1) Definition of indicators.
2) Data source(s).
3) Methods of data collection.
4) Frequency of data collection.
5) Responsibilities: Who would be responsible for collecting/acquiring data?
6) Data analysis plans.
7) Plans for evaluations.
8) Plans for reporting/using performance information.

Purpose Of Monitoring: Monitoring is very important in project planning and implementation.

It is like watching where you are going while headed towards that desired destination; you can make adjustments as you go along, and ensure that you are on the right track, doing things right, and making adjustments where/when necessary.

- Monitoring should be executed by all individuals and institutions (stakeholders) who have an interest in the project. To efficiently implement a project, the people planning and implementing it should plan for all the interrelated stages from the beginning.
- Monitoring provides information that will be useful in:
  - Analysing the situation in the community and its project.
  - Determining whether the inputs (resources, investments, etc.) in the project are well utilised.
  - Identifying problems facing the community or project and finding solutions.
  - Ensuring all activities are carried out properly by the right people and on time.
  - Using lessons from one project experience on to another, and
  - Determining whether the way the project was planned is the most appropriate way of solving the problem at hand.

The Meaning Of Evaluation: Evaluation is the scientific and deliberate process of judging the value of what a project or programme has achieved, particularly concerning activities planned and overall objectives. It involves value judgment. Hence, it is different from monitoring (which is observation and reporting of observations).

Evaluation is a process that systematically and objectively assesses all the elements of a programme. For example, design, implementation, and results achieved are used to determine their overall worth or significance. The objective is to provide credible information for decision-makers to identify ways to achieve more of the desired results.

Broadly speaking, there are two main types of evaluation:
- **Performance Evaluations** focus on the quality-of-service delivery and the outcomes (results) achieved by a programme. They typically cover short-term and medium-term outcomes. For example, student achievement levels, or the number of welfare recipients who move into full-time work. They are carried out based on information regularly collected through the programme monitoring system. Performance evaluation is broader than monitoring. It attempts to determine whether the progress achieved is the result of the intervention or whether another explanation is responsible for the observed changes.
- **Impact Evaluations** look for changes in outcomes that can be directly attributed to the programme being evaluated. They estimate what would have occurred had beneficiaries not participated in the programme. The determination of causality between the programme and a specific outcome is the key feature that distinguishes impact evaluation from any other type of assessment.

Purpose Of Evaluation
- Evaluation is important to identify the constraints or bottlenecks that hinder the project from achieving its objectives. Solutions to the constraints can then be proffered and implemented.
- Demonstrate how you will measure the outcomes of your project by;
  - ✓ Describe how you will collect your evaluation information.
  - ✓ How the data will be analysed.

- ✓ How/whether to include/use qualitative and quantitative data.
- ➢ Evaluation also enables the project planners and implementers to assess the benefits and costs that accrue to the intended direct and indirect beneficiaries of the project.
- ➢ Evaluation is essential for drawing lessons from the project implementation experience/experiences and using the lessons in the planning of other projects in that community and elsewhere.
- ➢ Finally, evaluation should provide a clear picture of the extent to which the intended objectives of the activities and the project have been realised.

The Process Of Evaluation: When should/do we do the evaluation?

Evaluation can and should be done: (a) before, (b) during, and (c) after implementation.

A) Before project implementation, evaluation is needed to:
- ✓ Assess the possible consequences of the planned project(s) to the people in the community over a period.
- ✓ Make a final decision on which project alternative should be implemented, and
- ✓ Assist in making decisions on how the project will be implemented.

B) During project implementation:
- ✓ Evaluation should be a continuous process and should take place in all project implementation activities and phases. This enables the project planners and implementers to progressively review the project strategies according to the changing circumstances to attain the desired activity and project objectives.

C) After project implementation:

This is to retrace the project planning and implementation process and results after project implementation. This further helps in:
- ✓ Identifying constraints or bottlenecks inherent in the implementation phase.
- ✓ Assessing the actual benefits and the number of people who benefited.
- ✓ Providing ideas on the strength of the project, for replication, and

✓ Providing a clear picture of the extent to which the intended objectives of the project have been realised.

Who Is An Administrator?

➢ Manager in an organisation: somebody whose job is to manage the affairs of a business, organisation, or institution.

➢ Somebody who handles or controls something, especially somebody who works skilfully.

Microsoft® Encarta® © Microsoft Corporation. All rights reserved.

Administrators' Duties And Responsibilities

➢ Manage resources.

➢ Ensure quality (Quality Assurance).

➢ Maintain agreed standards.

➢ Supervise other team players (within his/her jurisdiction).

Who Is A Manager?

Managers are responsible for the processes of getting activities completed efficiently with and through other people and setting and achieving the firm's goals through the execution of four basic management functions: planning, organising, leading, and controlling.

A manager is a person who manages a team of employees in an organisation. Often, managers get the work done through the employees and make sure the decorum of the organisation is maintained. A manager builds a bridge between the employees and the top-level management.

At the most fundamental level, management is a discipline that consists of a set of five general functions: planning, organising, staffing, leading, and controlling. These five functions are part of a body of practices and theories on how to be a successful manager.

Summary Of Monitoring & Evaluation Definitions:

Monitoring

- Clarifies programme objectives.
- Link project activities to their resources and objectives.
- Translate into measurable indicators/set targets.
- Collect data on indicators.
- Progress report.

Evaluation

- Analyses of how intended results were/were not achieved.
- Assesses contributions of activities to results.
- Examines results not easily measured.
- Explores unintended results.
- Provides lessons learned and recommendations.

What Monitoring and Evaluation have in common is that they are geared towards learning from what you are doing and how you are doing it, by focusing on:

- **Efficiency**: tells you that the input into the work is appropriate in terms of the output. This could be input in terms of money, time, staff, equipment, and so on. When you run a project and are concerned about its replicability or about scaling up, it is very important to get the efficiency element right.

- **Effectiveness**: is a measure of the extent to which a development programme/project achieves the specific objectives it set. If, for example, we set out to improve the quality (qualifications, exposure, knowledge, etc) of all the secondary school teachers in a particular district, did we succeed?

- **Impact**: tells you whether or not what you did made a difference to the problem situation you were trying to address. In other words, was your strategy useful? Was the intervention successful? Did ensuring that teachers were better qualified improve the pass rate of the final-year students at schools? Before you decide to get bigger or to replicate the project elsewhere, you need to be sure that what you are doing makes sense in terms of the impact you want to achieve.

Monitoring and Evaluation offer a tangible way to ensure that your project is accountable, transparent, minimises collateral damage, and actively identifies wasteful processes and poor performance.

Common Myths About Evaluation

- An evaluation must be large-scale.
- An evaluation must be sophisticated.
- An evaluation must involve a consultant.
- Evaluation is difficult.
- Evaluation is a threat.
- It means more work.
- Evaluation is merely an academic exercise.
- Many people believe that Monitoring and Evaluation is a useless activity that generates lots of boring data with useless conclusions.
- Some people also believe that Monitoring and Evaluation is about proving the success or failure of a programme. This myth assumes that success is implementing the perfect programme and never having to hear from employees, customers, or clients. Whereas success is remaining open to continuing feedback and adjusting the programme accordingly. Evaluation gives you this continuing feedback.
- Many also believe that Monitoring and Evaluation is a highly unique and complex process that occurs at a certain time in a certain way, and almost always includes the use of outside experts.

ACTIVITY

- Draw up a chart of your organisation's administrative system and processes.
- What are the core duties of each administrator?

CHAPTER TWO (2) – PLANNING, DESIGNING & IMPLEMENTATION

A Brief Introduction

The concept of programme Monitoring and Evaluation can include a wide variety of methods to evaluate many aspects of projects/programmes, both in non-profit and for-profit organisations.

Of course, and without doubt, numerous books and articles provide in-depth analysis of Monitoring and Evaluation, their designs, methods, tools, and combinations of methods and techniques of analysis.

As they say, "Half bread is better than none." As such, it is always better to do what might turn out to be an average effort at Monitoring and Evaluation than not to evaluate at all. Besides, if you resort to bringing in an evaluation consultant, you should be a smart consumer. Monitoring and Evaluation must be carried out realistically and practically.

Programme Versus Project

However, for this material, both "project" and "programme" would be used interchangeably. The following are the popular clarifications and similarities between both concepts.

- A programme is ongoing and implemented within a business to consistently achieve certain results for the business. A project is designed to deliver an output or deliverable, and its success will be in terms of delivering the right output at the right time and at the right cost.

- The primary difference between these two roles is scope and ambiguity: Projects are scoped tightly and controlled from the beginning, while programmes have a larger scope that may change throughout the programme.

- Projects are temporary endeavours to accomplish something specific, while a programme is the repetitive management of the end result of the project.

Programmes are sometimes made up of multiple ongoing or completed projects that are managed together.

In summary, a project represents a single, focused effort. Programmes are collections of projects that constitute a complete package of work. The programme's overall objectives are achieved through the complementarity of the various projects; they are both concerned with change, that is, the creation of something new, and both require the use of a team to get things done.

What Is Programme/Project Evaluation?

Typically, organisations work from their mission to identify several overall goals that must be reached to accomplish their mission. In non-profit organisations, for example, each of these goals often becomes a programme. Non-profit programmes are organised methods to provide certain related services to constituents, for example, students, teachers, clients, patients, etc. These programmes must be evaluated to decide if the programmes are indeed useful to constituents.

Programme evaluation is carefully collecting information about a programme or some aspect of a programme in order to make necessary decisions about the programme.

The type of evaluation you undertake to improve your programme depends on what you want to learn about the programme.

Planning For Monitoring And Evaluation

Monitoring and Evaluation should be part of your planning process. When you do your planning process, you will set and use indicators. These indicators provide the framework for your Monitoring and Evaluation system. They tell you:

- What you and the recipient of the report (project/programme owners) want to and should know.
- Kinds of information that will be useful to collect.
- How will we get information?
- Who should be involved?

Planning your project/programme, Monitoring and Evaluation depend on what information you need to make your decisions and on your resources.

- ➤ Often, management wants to know everything about their products, services, or programmes. However, limited resources usually force managers to prioritise what they need to know to make decisions.
- ➤ Your programme/project evaluation plans depend on what information you need to collect to make major decisions.
- ➤ But the more focused you are about what you want to examine by the evaluation, the more efficient you can be in your evaluation, the shorter the time it will take you and ultimately the less it will cost you (whether in your own time, the time of your employees and/or the time of a consultant).
- ➤ There are trade-offs, too, in the breadth and depth of information you get. The more breadth you want, usually the less depth you get. On the other hand, if you want to examine a certain aspect of a programme in great detail, you will likely not get as much information about other aspects of the programme.

Key Considerations:

- ➤ For what purposes is the evaluation being done? That is, what do you want to be able to decide as a result of the evaluation?
- ➤ Who are the audiences for the information from the evaluation? For example, customers, bankers, funders, board, management, staff, clients, etc.?
- ➤ What kinds of information are needed to make the decision you need to make and/or enlighten your intended audiences?
- ➤ From which sources should the information be collected? For example, employees, customers, clients, groups of customers or clients, etc.?
- ➤ How can that information be collected reasonably? For instance, questionnaires, interviews, observing customers, etc.?
- ➤ When is the information needed, and by when must it be collected?
- ➤ What resources are available to collect the information?

Some Major Types Of Evaluation

When designing your evaluation approach, it may be helpful to review the following three (3) types of evaluations, which are rather common in organisations.

Note that you should not design your Monitoring and Evaluation approach simply by choosing which of the following three (3) types you will use; you should design your Monitoring and Evaluation approach by carefully addressing the key considerations above.

1) Goals-Based Evaluation

Here, Monitoring and Evaluation programmes are established to meet one or more specific goals. These goals are often described in the original programme plans. Goal-based evaluations evaluate the extent to which programmes are meeting predetermined goals or objectives.

Questions to ask yourself when designing an evaluation to see if you reached your goals are:

- ✓ How were the programme goals established?
- ✓ Was the process effective?
- ✓ What is the status of the programme's progress toward achieving the goals?
- ✓ Will the goals be achieved according to the timelines specified in the programme implementation or operations plan? If not, then why?
- ✓ Do we have adequate resources (money, training, etc.) to achieve the goals?
- ✓ How should priorities be changed to put more focus on achieving the goals?
- ✓ How should timelines be changed? Know why efforts are behind before timelines are changed.
- ✓ How should goals be changed? Be careful about making these changes and know why efforts are not achieving the goals before changing them.
- ✓ Should any goal be added or removed? Why?
- ✓ How should goals be established in the future?

2) Process-Based Evaluations

Process-based evaluations are geared toward fully understanding how a programme works. These evaluations are useful if programmes are long-standing and have changed over the years, employees or customers report a large number of complaints about the programme, or there are inefficiencies. Numerous questions might be addressed in a process evaluation.

- ✓ On what basis do employees and/or customers decide that products or services are needed?
- ✓ What is required of employees to deliver the product or services?
- ✓ How are employees trained on how to deliver the product or services?
- ✓ How do customers or clients come into the programme?
- ✓ What is required of customers or clients?
- ✓ How do employees select which products or services will be provided to the customer or client?
- ✓ What is the general process that customers or clients go through with the product or programme?
- ✓ What do customers or clients consider to be strengths of the programme?
- ✓ What do staff consider to be strengths of the product or programme?
- ✓ What typical complaints are heard from employees and/or customers?
- ✓ What do employees and/or customers recommend improving in the product or programme?
- ✓ On what basis do employees and/or the customer decide that the product or services are no longer needed?

3) **Outcome-Based Evaluation**: Programme Monitoring and Evaluation with an outcome focus is increasingly important. An outcome-based evaluation facilitates your asking if your organisation is doing the right programme to bring about the outcomes you need.

The general steps to accomplishing an outcome-based evaluation include.

- a) Identify the major outcomes that you want to examine or verify for the programme under evaluation.
- b) Choose the outcomes that you want to examine, prioritise the outcomes, and, if your time and resources are limited, pick the top two to four most important outcomes to examine for now.

c) For each outcome, specify what observable measures or indicators will suggest that you are achieving that key outcome with your clients.

d) Specify a "target" goal for clients. That is, what number or percentage of clients do you commit to achieving specific outcomes with?

e) Identify what information is needed to show these indicators.

f) Decide how that information can be efficiently and realistically gathered.

g) Analyse and report the findings.

CHAPTER THREE (3) – DESIGNING AN EFFECTIVE M&E

High-performing teams/units take a rigorous and disciplined approach to conducting performance evaluations. Good performance evaluations require committed leaders, courageous supervisors, and open employees.

Although this aspect of this handbook will still be examined in greater technical detail in a later chapter, here are some basic things you need to know about an Evaluation Plan.

What Is A Monitoring And Evaluation Plan?

A Monitoring and Evaluation (M&E) plan is a document that helps to track and assess the results of the interventions throughout the life of a program. It is a living document that should be referred to and updated regularly. While the specifics of each project/programme's Monitoring and Evaluation plan will look different, they should all follow the same basic structure and include the same key elements.

A Monitoring and Evaluation plan will include some documents that may have been created during the programme/project planning process and some that will need to be created. For example, elements such as the logic model/logical framework, Theory of Change (ToC), and monitoring indicators may have already been developed with input from key stakeholders and/or the programme donor. The Monitoring and Evaluation plan takes those documents and develops a further plan for their implementation.

Why Develop A Monitoring And Evaluation Plan?

It is important to develop a Monitoring and Evaluation plan before beginning any monitoring activity so that there is a clear plan for what questions about the programme need to be answered. It will help programme staff decide how they are going to collect data to track indicators, how monitoring data will be analysed, and how the results of data collection will be disseminated both to the donor and internally among staff members for programme improvement.

Remember, Monitoring and Evaluation data alone is not useful until someone puts it to use! A Monitoring and Evaluation plan will help make sure data is being used efficiently to make programs as effective as possible and to be able to report on results at the end of the programme.

Selecting Which Evaluation Method To Use

The overall goal in selecting evaluation method(s) is to get the most useful information to key decision-makers, most cost-effectively and realistically.

Consider the following questions:

- What information is needed to make current decisions about a product or programme/project?
- Of this information, how much can be collected and analysed in a low-cost and practical manner? For example, using questionnaires, surveys, and checklists.
- How accurate will the information be?
- Will the methods get all the needed information?
- What additional methods should and could be used?
- Will the information be credible to decision-makers like top management?
- Will the nature of the audience conform to the methods? For example, will they fill out questionnaires carefully, engage in interviews or focus groups, let you examine their documentation, etc.?
- Who can administer the methods now, or is training required?
- How can the information be analysed?

Note that, ideally, the evaluator uses a combination of methods. For example, a questionnaire, to quickly collect a great deal of information from a lot of people, and then interviews are conducted to get more in-depth information from certain respondents to the questionnaires. Perhaps case studies could then be used for more in-depth analysis of unique and notable cases. For example, those who benefited or did not benefit from the programme, those who quit the programme, etc.

Four Levels Of Evaluation:

There are four levels of Monitoring and Evaluation information that can be gathered:

1. **Reactions and feelings**: feelings are often poor indicators that your service made a lasting impact.
2. **Learning**: enhanced attitudes, perceptions, or knowledge.
3. **Changes in skills**: applied the learning to enhance behaviours.
4. **Effectiveness**: improved performance because of enhanced behaviours.

Usually, the farther your evaluation information gets down the list, the more useful your evaluation is.

Who Should Carry Out The Evaluation?

➤ Ideally, management decides what the evaluation goals should be. Then an evaluation expert helps the organisation to determine what the evaluation methods should be, and how the resulting data will be analysed and reported back to the organisation.

➤ If no outside help can be obtained, the organisation can still learn a great deal by applying the methods and analysing the results itself. However, there is a strong chance that data about the strengths and weaknesses of a programme will not be interpreted fairly if the data are analysed by the people responsible for ensuring the programme is a good one.

Analysing And Interpreting Information

Analysing quantitative and qualitative data is often the topic of advanced research and evaluation methodology. Certain basics can help to make sense of reams of data.

Always start with your evaluation goals: When analysing data (whether from questionnaires, interviews, focus groups, or whatever), always start with a review of your evaluation goals, that is, the reason you undertook the evaluation in the first place. This will help you organise your data and focus your analysis. For example, if you want to improve your programme by identifying its strengths and weaknesses, you can organise data into programme strengths, weaknesses, and suggestions to improve the programme. If you want to fully understand how your programme works, you could organise data in chronological order in which clients go through your programme. If you are conducting an outcome-based evaluation, you can categorise data according to the indicators for each outcome.

Basic analysis of "quantitative" information (for information other than commentary). For example, ratings, rankings, yeses, nos, etc.
- ✓ Make copies of your data and store the master copy away. Use the copy for making edits, cutting and pasting, etc.
- ✓ Tabulate the information. That is, add up the number of ratings, rankings, yeses, and nos for each question.
- ✓ For ratings and rankings, consider computing a mean, or average, for each question. For example, "For question #1, the average ranking was 2.4". This is more meaningful than indicating, for example, how many respondents ranked 1, 2, or 3.
- ✓ Consider conveying the range of answers, for example, 20 people ranked "1", 30 ranked "2", and 20 people ranked "3".

Basic analysis of "qualitative" information (respondents' verbal answers in interviews, focus groups, or written commentary on questionnaires):
- ✓ Read through all the data.
- ✓ Organise comments into similar categories. For example, concerns, suggestions, strengths, weaknesses, similar experiences, programme inputs, recommendations, outputs, outcome indicators, etc.
- ✓ Label the categories or themes. For example, concerns, suggestions, etc.
- ✓ Attempt to identify patterns, associations, and causal relationships in the themes. For example, "All people who attended the programme in the evening had similar concerns", "most people came from the same geographic area", "most people were in the same salary range", "what processes or events respondents experience during the programme", etc.

✓ Keep (store) all commentary for several years after completion in case needed for future reference.

Interpreting Information:

✓ Attempt to put the information in perspective. For example, compare results to what you expected, promised results:

- Management or programme staff; any common standards for your services; original programme goals (especially if you are conducting a programme evaluation).
- Indications of accomplishing outcomes (especially if you are conducting an outcomes evaluation).
- Description of the programme's experiences, strengths, weaknesses, etc. (especially if you are conducting a process evaluation).

✓ Consider recommendations to help programme staff improve the programme, conclusions about programme operations, or meeting goals, etc.

✓ Record conclusions and recommendations in a report document, and associate interpretations to justify your conclusions or recommendations.

Reporting Evaluation Results

✓ The level and scope of content depend on whom the report is intended for – bankers, funders/sponsors, employees, customers, clients, the public, etc.

✓ Be sure employees have a chance to carefully review and discuss the report. Translate recommendations to action plans, including who is going to do what about the programme and by when (timelines and schedules).

✓ Bankers or funders will likely require a report that includes an Executive Summary (this is a summary of conclusions and recommendations, not a listing of what sections of information are in the report); a description of the organisation and the programme under evaluation, an explanation of the evaluation goals, methods, and analysis procedures, listing of conclusions and recommendations, and any relevant attachments. For example, the inclusion of evaluation questionnaires, interview guides, etc. The banker or funder may want the report to be delivered as a presentation, accompanied by an overview of the report, or the banker or funder may want to review the report alone.

✓ Be sure to record the evaluation plans and activities in an evaluation plan that can be referenced when a similar programme evaluation is needed in the future.

Contents Of An Evaluation Plan: Things to consider to be included in and done when planning for an evaluation, include, but are not limited to:

➢ It is essential to develop an evaluation plan to ensure your programme evaluations are carried out efficiently in the future.

➢ Ensure your evaluation plan is documented, so you can regularly and efficiently carry out your evaluation activities.

➢ Record enough information in the plan so that someone outside of the organisation, at least other than you, can understand what you are evaluating and how.

Consider the following format for your evaluation report:

1. Title page (name of the organisation that is being, or has a product, service, or programme that is being, evaluated, date).
2. Table of contents.
3. Executive summary (one-page, concise overview of findings and recommendations).
4. Purpose of the report (what type of evaluation was conducted, what decisions are being aided by the findings of the evaluation, who is making the decision, etc.).
5. Background about the organisation and product, service, and programme that is being evaluated.
   a) Organisation's description and history.
      Product/Service/Programme description (that is being evaluated).
   b) Problem statement (in the case of a non-profit, description of the community need that is being met by the product/service/programme).
   c) Overall goal(s) of Product/Service/Programme.

    d) Outcomes (or client/customer impacts) and performance measures (that can be measured as indicators of the outcomes).

    e) Activities/Technologies of the Product/Service/Programme (general description of how the product/service/programme is developed and delivered).

    f) Staffing (description of the number of personnel and roles in the organisation that are relevant to developing and delivering the product/service/programme).

6. Overall evaluation goals. For example, what questions are being answered by the evaluation?

7. Methodology.

    a. Types of data/information that were collected.

    b. How data/information was collected (what instruments were used, etc.).

    c. How data/information was analysed.

    d. Limitations of the evaluation (for example, cautions about findings/conclusions and how to use the findings/conclusions, etc.).

8. Interpretations and Conclusions (from analysis of the data/information).

9. Recommendations (regarding the decisions that must be made about the product/service/programme).

Appendices: The content of the appendices depends on the goals of the evaluation report. For example,

    a. Instruments used to collect data/information.

    b. Data, for example, in tabular format, etc.

    c. Testimonials, comments made by users of the product/service/programme.

    d. Case studies of users of the product/service/programme.

    e. Any related literature.

Hitches, Successes, and Strategies

Pitfalls to Avoid

- Do not baulk at evaluation because it seems far too "scientific." It is not. Usually, the first 20% of the effort will generate 80% of the plan, and this is far better than nothing.
- There is no "perfect" evaluation design. Do not worry about the plan being perfect. It is far more important to do something than to wait until every detail has been tested.
- Work hard to include some interviews in your evaluation methods. Questionnaires do not capture "the story," and the story is usually the most powerful depiction of the benefits of your services.
- Do not interview just the successes. You will learn a great deal about the programme by understanding its failures, dropouts, etc.
- Do not throw away evaluation results once a report has been generated. Results do not take up much room, and they can provide precious information later when trying to understand changes in the programme.

Strategies For Success Of An Evaluation

- Focus on the key results.
- Gather peer and manager input.
- Link measures to impacts.
- Measure outcomes rather than outputs.
- Identify up front how to best measure results.
- Use feedback ratings.
- Provide appropriate resources and authority.
- Set challenging performance expectations.
- Set stretch goals.
- Set the bar at excellence.
- Prepare: Identify key issues/themes that need to be discussed. Give employees a draft evaluation with enough time to review and come prepared for the evaluation conference.
- Avoid surprises: The evaluation conference should not be the first time an employee hears about a performance problem or receives recognition for an accomplishment.

- Be specific: Clearly explain accomplishments and failures. Refer to the deliverables in the performance plan. Describe the impact of achievements or performance issues.
- Be balanced: Document both good and bad performances. Capture specific awards and commendations, as well as corrective or disciplinary action and performance improvement plans. Make sure to evaluate the entire year and avoid the "Halo/horn effect" of evaluating only the most recent performance.
- Be succinct: Focus on the key deliverables and issues. Avoid details that do not pertain to the employee's performance.
- Be constructive: Focus on what the employee needs to do next to either develop knowledge and skills or improve performance.
- Provide supervisor training.
- Provide HR support to supervisors.
- Build a culture that values feedback.
- Monitor and review evaluations.
- Use 360-degree reviews.
- Have second-line supervisors review draft evaluations.
- Have supervisors of similar work units develop evaluations collaboratively.
- Have supervisors and employees develop evaluations collaboratively.

Potential Challenges

- Overloading supervisors.
- Employee resistance.
- Lack of executive support.
- History of not addressing poor performance.
- Identifying new and/or meaningful measures.
- Keeping measures simple.

Bottlenecks And Hitches

Not everyone will be pleased about any changes in plans you decide that need to be made. People often resist change. Some of the reasons for this include:

➤ People are comfortable with things the way they are – they do not want to be pushed out of their comfort zones.

➤ People worry that any change will lessen their levels of productivity – they feel judged by what they do and how much they do and do not want to take the time necessary to change plans or ways of doing things.

➤ People do not like to rush into change – how do we know that something different will be better? They spend so long thinking about it that it may become too late for useful changes to be made.

➤ People do not have the "big picture". They know what they are doing, and they can see it is working, so they cannot see any reason to change anything at all.

➤ People do not have a long-term commitment to the project or the organisation – they see it as a stepping stone on their career path. They do not want change because it will delay the items, they want to be able to tick off on their curriculum vitae (resumes).

➤ People feel they cannot cope – they have to keep doing what they are doing, but also work at bringing about change. It is all too much.

Dealing With Bottlenecks And Hitches

➤ Make the reasons why change is needed very clear – take people through the findings and conclusions of the Monitoring and Evaluation processes and involve them in decision-making.

➤ Help people see the whole picture, beyond their little bit, to the overall impact on the problem analysed.

➤ Focus on the key issues – "We have to do something about this!"

➤ Recognise anger, fear, and resistance.

➤ Listen to people and allow them to express frustration and other emotions.

➤ Find common ground – things that they also want to see changed.

➤ Encourage a feeling that change is exciting, that it frees people from doing things that are not working, so they can try new things that are likely to work, and that it releases productive energy.

➤ Emphasise the importance of everyone being committed to making it work.

➢ Create conditions for regular interaction – anything from a seminar to graffiti on a notice board, or even a retreat - to discuss what is happening and how.

CHAPTER FOUR (4) – EVALUATION TYPES AND MODELS

Model evaluation is the process of using different evaluation metrics to understand a machine learning model's performance, as well as its strengths and weaknesses. Model evaluation is important to assess the efficacy of a model during initial research phases, and it also plays a role in model monitoring.

Comparison of actual project impacts against the agreed strategic plans looks at;

> What have you set out to achieve?

> What have you accomplished?

> How did you accomplish it?

Broadly, evaluation can be formative or summative but can further be sub-categorised. Whatever the evaluation type (formative or summative), evaluation always looks at;

> Effectiveness.

> Efficiency.

> Impact.

> Relevance.

> Sustainability.

Types Of Evaluative Models

Formative Evaluation Model: Strengthens or improves the object(s) being evaluated. They help by examining:

> The delivery of the programme or technology.

> The quality of its implementation.

> The assessment of the organisational context, personnel, procedures, and inputs.

Summative Evaluation Model: Examines the effects or outcomes of some objects.

> Summative evaluations examine the effects or outcomes of interventions.

- ➤ They determine the overall impact of the causal factor beyond only the immediate target outcomes.
- ➤ They estimate the relative costs of the project.

'Pre-Test' – 'Post-Test' Model: Assumes the situation will change following the intervention deployed.

Comparison Group Model: Compare a group that has had the intervention to a group that did not.

Types of Summative Evaluation

- ✓ Outcome evaluation investigates whether the intervention caused demonstrable effects on specifically defined target outcomes.
- ✓ Impact evaluation assesses the overall or net effects, intended or unintended, of the intervention.
- ✓ Cost-Effectiveness and Cost-Benefit Analysis addresses efficiency by standardising outcomes in terms of their dollar costs and values.
- ✓ Secondary Analysis re-examines existing data to address new questions or use methods not previously employed.
- ✓ Meta-analysis integrates the outcome estimates from multiple studies to arrive at an overall or summary judgment on an evaluation question.

Types Of Evaluation: The following are the different types of evaluation;

Self-Evaluation

- ✓ The organisation decides to check (assess) itself by looking inwards and assessing how it is doing/performing.
- ✓ Only an organisation interested in success can honestly do this.

Participatory Evaluation

- ✓ Also, a form of internal evaluation.

✓ It involves the frontline staff, or the people directly related to the project. That is, project staff and the beneficiaries, since they work together on the project – it is their participation that forms the nucleus and core of the project, and they determine the outcome of the evaluation together.

Rapid Participatory Appraisal (RPA)

✓ It is a semi-structured evaluation carried out over a short time.

✓ Used as a starting point for understanding the local situation.

✓ Involves the use of already existing information collected by other organisations or projects.

✓ Involves the use of data review, direct observation, group interviews, and valuable input from beneficiaries of the intervention.

✓ It is a flexible and interactive evaluation type.

✓ A quick way of getting information.

External Evaluation: This evaluation is conducted by a carefully chosen external team or individual, a consultant.

Interactive Evaluation

✓ Active interaction between the external evaluation team and the organisation's project/programme team works together for this type of evaluation.

✓ You may sometimes include an insider, who may not be directly involved in the project, as part of this evaluation team.

Evaluation Tools

✓ Interviews.

✓ Key Informant Interviews (KIIS).

✓ Questionnaires.

✓ Focus Groups.

✓ Community Meetings.

✓ Fieldworker Reports.

✓ Ranking.

- ✓ Visual/Audio Stimuli.
- ✓ Rating Scales.
- ✓ Critical Event/Incident Analysis.

Levels Of Baseline Data: Baseline data are the initial data collected before the start of an intervention. These data serve as a point of reference as subsequent data are collected and compared against the baseline data to measure progress towards intervention goals.

- ✓ **General Information**: Generally available information, such as official statistics, for example, literacy rates, school gender enrolment, etc.
- ✓ **Specific Information**: If we are working with specific people or organisations. For example, the number of people/classrooms, and the percentage of national exam success in the school.
- ✓ **Intake Information**: If the project is with individuals, we need information like age, gender, and education level. Information may be obtained through interviews and questionnaires.

Damage Control

- ✓ Done if Baseline data was not done (collected) before intervention.
- ✓ Use anecdotal information from people who were around at the beginning of the project.
- ✓ Use control groups.

Key Outcome And Impact Evaluation Indicators For School Administration

- ✓ Process outcomes.
- ✓ School access outcomes.
- ✓ Quality of education outcomes.
- ✓ Student achievement outcomes.

Process Outcomes

- ✓ Improvement in security, infrastructure, and equipment.
- ✓ Has there been teaching and curricular innovation?

- ✓ With the change, have teaching practices changed?
- ✓ Has there been managerial training for teachers?
- ✓ Is there community and PTA (Parents Teachers Association) involvement in school activities?

Teacher Effort And Performance Evaluation

Teacher Survey

- ✓ Questionnaires on the level of interaction amongst teachers.
- ✓ Teacher motivation.
- ✓ How is the absenteeism of students dealt with?

Student Survey about Teacher Behaviour

- ✓ Do teachers endeavour to teach again what is not understood?
- ✓ Do teachers encourage students to read?
- ✓ Do teachers encourage teamwork and discussions in class?

School Access Outcomes

- ✓ Total school enrolment.
- ✓ Number of days students attend school compared to the number of days the school is open.

Quality of Education Outcomes

- ✓ Dropout rate.
- ✓ Promotion rate.
- ✓ Proportion of overage students- more likely to drop out.
- ✓ Student passing rates.

Activity

Student/pupil academic performance rates are to be increased in light of deplorable results in the last ten (10) years in public schools in the State.

- ✓ What are the main objectives of this exercise?

✓ How would you achieve these objectives?

CHAPTER FIVE (5) – INDICATORS

An indicator is a means of measuring actual results against planned or expected results in terms of quantity, quality, and timeliness. Indicators are markers of your project's achievements in a specific area. They describe a value that you want to achieve.

In Monitoring and Evaluation, indicators are measurable values that provide information about the performance of a project. They are used to measure progress towards goals, track changes in the environment, and assess the impact of the project.

The indicators are clues, signs, or markers that can be used to gauge the progress of a programme in achieving its desired outcome and can indicate the distance it is from reaching that goal.

What Are Indicators In Monitoring And Evaluation?

Indicators in Monitoring and Evaluation are measures that help to track and assess the progress and performance of a programme/project or intervention. They are specific, measurable, and observable characteristics or features that provide information about the inputs, activities, outputs, outcomes, and impact of the programme or intervention.

Indicators can be quantitative or qualitative and are used to measure changes over time and assess the effectiveness of interventions. They help to answer important questions such as:

- ✓ Is the programme or intervention reaching its intended target audience?
- ✓ Are the programme activities being implemented as planned?
- ✓ Is the programme achieving its desired outcomes?
- ✓ What impact is the programme having on the target population?

Indicators in Monitoring and Evaluation are selected based on the specific goals and objectives of the programme or intervention being evaluated. They should be regularly tracked and reported to assess progress and inform decision-making about programme/project improvement.

Types Of Indicators In Monitoring And Evaluation

In general, indicators are specific, measurable, and observable data points that are used to monitor and evaluate progress towards achieving specific goals and objectives. Indicators are essential components of Monitoring and Evaluation, as they provide a basis for measuring progress, identifying successes and challenges, and informing decision-making.

Several types of indicators can be used in Monitoring and Evaluation, these include:

- ✓ **Input Indicators**: These measure the resources invested in a programme or project, such as the amount of funding, staff time, or materials.
- ✓ **Output Indicators**: These measure the direct results or products of a programme or project, such as the number of people reached, the number of services delivered, or the number of products produced.
- ✓ **Outcome Indicators**: These indicator types measure the changes or impacts that result from a programme or project, such as improvements in health, education, or income.
- ✓ **Process Indicators**: These measure how well a programme or project is being implemented, such as the quality of services provided, the timeliness of delivery, or the level of stakeholder engagement.
- ✓ **Impact Indicators**: Long-term, enduring effects of a programme or project on a population or environment can be measured with the use of impact indicators, a specific sort of performance indicator.
- ✓ **Efficiency Indicators**: These measure the cost-effectiveness of a programme or project, such as the ratio of resources invested to results achieved.
- ✓ **Effectiveness Indicators**: These measure the extent to which a programme or project is achieving its objectives, such as the proportion of the target population reached.
- ✓ **Quality Indicators**: These measure the quality of the programme or project delivery, such as the satisfaction levels of beneficiaries.
- ✓ **Sustainability Indicators**: These measure the potential for a programme or project to continue after external support has ended, such as the degree to which local communities are involved in the programme or project.

Indicators should be **SMART**, which means they should be Specific, Measurable, Achievable, Relevant, and Time-bound. Also, they should be clearly defined, measurable, achievable within a reasonable timeframe, relevant to the goals and objectives of the programme or project, and have a set timeframe for measurement.

When selecting indicators, it is important to involve key stakeholders, consider the availability of data and resources, and select indicators that are meaningful and relevant to the context and goals of the programme or project.

Tips for the Development of Indicators: The tips below apply to indicators of all projects.

- ✓ **Relevance**: Indicators should be relevant to the needs of the user and the purpose of monitoring. They should be able to indicate to the user whether progress is being made (or not) in addressing the problems identified.

- ✓ **Disaggregation**: Data should be disaggregated according to what is to be measured. For example, for individuals, the basic disaggregation is by sex (gender), age group, level of education, and other personal characteristics useful to understanding how the programme functions. For services and/or programmes, the disaggregation is normally done by type of service/programme and comprehensibility. Indicators should be easy to use and understand, and data for their calculation should be relatively simple to collect.

- ✓ **Clarity of definition**: A vaguely defined indicator will be open to several interpretations and may be measured in different ways at different times and places. It is useful in this regard to include the source of data to be used and calculation examples/methods.

For example, the indicator "employment of participants at follow-up" will require:

(i)	Specification of what constitutes employment (work for at least one hour for pay, profit, or in kind in the 10 days before the measurement);
(ii)	A definition of participants (for example, those who attended at least 50 per cent of the programme); and,
(iii)	A follow-up timeframe (six months after the completion of the programme). Care must also be taken in defining the standard or

benchmark of comparison. For example, in examining the status of young people, what constitutes the norm – the situation of youth in a particular region or at a national level?

✓ **The number chosen should be small**: There are no hard and fast rules to determine the appropriate number of indicators. However, a rule of thumb is that users should avoid two temptations: information overload and over-aggregation (that is, too much data and designing a composite index based on aggregation and weighting schemes, which may conceal important information). A common mistake is to over-engineer a monitoring system (for example, the collection of data for hundreds of indicators, most of which are not used). In the field of employment programmes, senior officials tend to make use of high-level strategic indicators such as outputs and outcomes. Line managers and their staff, conversely, focus on operational indicators that target processes and services.

✓ **Specificity**: The selection of indicators should reflect those problems that the youth employment programme intends to address. For example, a programme aimed at providing work experience to early school leavers needs to incorporate indicators on coverage (how many among all school leavers participate in the programme), the type of enterprises where the work experience takes place and the occupation, and number of beneficiaries that obtain a job afterwards by individual characteristics (for example, sex, educational attainment, household status and so on).

✓ **Cost**: There is a trade-off between indicators and the cost of collecting data for their measurement. If the collection of data becomes too expensive and time-consuming, the indicator may ultimately lose its relevance.

✓ **Technical soundness**: Data should be reliable. The user should be informed about how the indicators were constructed and the sources used. A short discussion should be provided about their meaning, interpretation, and, most importantly, their limitations. Indicators must be available on a timely basis, especially if they are to provide feedback during programme implementation.

✓ **Forward-looking**: A well-designed system of indicators must not be restricted to conveying information about current concerns. Indicators must also measure trends over time.

✓ **Adaptability**: Indicators should be readily adaptable to use in different regions and circumstances.

Source: adapted from Canadian International Development Agency (CIDA), 1997. Guide to Gender-Sensitive Indicators (Ottawa, CIDA).

Performance Indicators: Performance indicators are measures of project impacts, outcomes, outputs, and inputs that are monitored during project implementation to assess progress toward project objectives. They are also used later to evaluate a project's success. The following are characteristics that such indicators should have and perform:

✓ Measures of inputs, processes, outputs, and impacts for projects or strategies.
✓ Must be supported by sound data collection to be successful.
✓ Enables managers to track progress, demonstrate results, and take corrective actions to improve service delivery.

Uses

✓ Setting performance targets and assessing progress towards achieving them.
✓ Identify problems via an early warning system to allow corrective action to be taken.
✓ Indicate whether an in-depth evaluation or review is needed.

Advantages

✓ Effective means to measure progress towards objectives.
✓ Facilitates benchmarking comparisons between different units.
✓ Facilitates benchmarking comparisons over time.

Disadvantages

✓ Poorly defined indicators are not good measures of success.
✓ Too many indicators make the system costly and likely to be underutilised.
✓ The trade-offs between picking the optimal indicators and indicators based on the data available.
✓ May not capture what is going on at the local level.
✓ May not take into account and consider the enabling environment.

✓ Broadly defined indicators can be subjective, leading to different interpretations.

Examples Of Indicators For Some Sectors:

Economic Indicators

✓ Average annual household income.

✓ Average weekly/monthly wages.

✓ Employment, by age group.

✓ Unemployment, by age group, by gender.

✓ Employment, by occupation, by gender.

✓ Government employment.

✓ Earned income levels.

✓ Average length of unemployment period.

✓ Default rates on loans.

✓ The ratio of homeowners to renters.

✓ Per capita income.

✓ Average annual family income.

✓ Percentage of people below the poverty line.

✓ The ratio of seasonal to permanent employment.

✓ The growth rate of small businesses.

✓ Value of residential construction and/or renovation.

Examples Of Socio-Economic Indicators

✓ Death rate.

✓ Life expectancy at birth.

✓ Infant mortality rates and causes of death.

✓ Number of nurses per capita.

✓ Literacy rates, by age and gender.

✓ Student: teacher ratios.

✓ Retention rate by school level.

✓ School completion rates by exit points.

✓ Public spending per student.

- ✓ Number of suicides.
- ✓ Causes of accidents.
- ✓ Infant mortality rate.
- ✓ Rates of HIV infection and deaths.
- ✓ Number of movie theatres/swimming pools per 1000 residents.
- ✓ Number of radios/televisions per family.
- ✓ Per capita.
- ✓ Availability of books in traditional languages and traditional languages taught in schools.
- ✓ Time spent listening to the radio/watching television by gender.

ACTIVITY

List at least twenty (20) indicators to be used for evaluation purposes in the area of need in your organisation.

CHAPTER SIX (6) – FRAMEWORKS

AN INTEGRAL COMPONENT OF THE PROJECT PLANNING & IMPLEMENTATION PROCESS

What Are Frameworks?

A framework is a tool that helps an organisation or an individual plan and execute Monitoring and Evaluation activities.

Planning effective Monitoring and Evaluation frameworks involves defining goals, objectives, and indicators to measure progress. The framework ensures that the data collected is relevant and helpful in making informed decisions.

For many organisations, a Monitoring and Evaluation framework is a table that describes the indicators that are used to measure whether the programme is a success.

- ➤ Frameworks are key elements of Monitoring and Evaluation plans that describe the components of a project and the sequence of steps required to achieve the desired outcomes.
- ➤ They help increase understanding of the programme's goals and objectives.
- ➤ They define the relationships between key factors to implementation.
- ➤ Delineate the internal and external elements that could affect its success.
- ➤ They are crucial for understanding and analysing how a programme is supposed to work.
- ➤ There is no one perfect framework, and no single framework is appropriate for all situations (project and programme).

Types of Frameworks

Conceptual Framework: Also called a "Research Framework," is useful for identifying and illustrating the factors and relationships that influence the outcome of a programme or intervention. They are typically shown as diagrams illustrating causal linkages between the key components of a programme and the outcomes of interest.

For instance, a programme, in addition to other donors, is supplying free training for teachers to increase service quality, with the ultimate outcome of improved education.

Results Framework: Also called "Strategic Framework," diagrams the direct causal relationships between the incremental results of the key activities up to the overall objective and goal of the intervention.

> In a result framework, an SO (Strategic Objective) is an outcome that is the most ambitious result that can be achieved and for which the organisation is willing to be held responsible.
> An IR (intermediate result) is a discrete result or outcome that is necessary to achieve an SO.

Log(ic) Model/Logical Framework: A log frame is a tool for improving the planning, implementation, management, monitoring, and evaluation of projects. The log frame is a way of structuring the main elements in a project and highlighting the logical linkages between them.

The Logical Framework is:

> A planning tool that sets out the objectives of a project and how they will be measured.
> They are the most commonly used tool in Monitoring and Evaluation and are favoured especially by funders/sponsors.
> A concise document.

It should be:

> Clear, readable, and jargon-free.
> Designed ideally with input from beneficiaries.
> The basis for Monitoring and Evaluation is later and hence kept under constant review.
> Filled in initially with the data you expect to find from the project.

> Completed at the halfway point/end of your project with the actual data collected.

Fig 6.1: Example of a logical framework

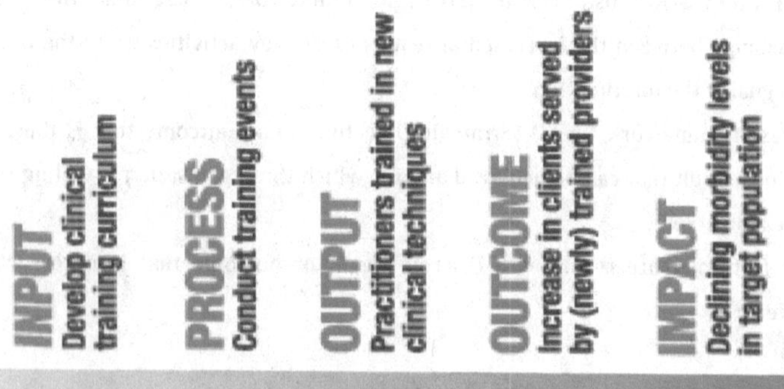

> A logic model, sometimes called a "Monitoring and Evaluation Framework", provides a streamlined linear interpretation of a project's planned use of resources and its desired ends.

Logic models have five essential components:

Inputs: The resources invested in a programme. For example, technical assistance, computers, textbooks, or training.

Processes: The activities carried out to achieve the objectives of the programme. For example, training of staff (teachers), purchase of key office equipment, and provision of technical assistance.

Outputs: The intermediate results achieved at the programme level through the execution of activities.

Outcomes: The set of short-term or immediate results at the population level achieved by the programme through the execution of activities.

Impacts: The long-term effects or results of the programme. For example, changes in academic results. In this context, the term "impact" refers to the students' examination results or conditions that the programme is intended ultimately to influence (examination results, employability, literacy, empowerment, etc.) as measured by several impact indicators.

- ✓ In plain words, inputs (or resources) are used in processes (or activities) which produce intermediate results (or outputs), ultimately leading to longer-term or broader results (or outcomes) and impacts.
- ✓ The example presents a straightforward view of a project designed to improve academic performance in schools by increasing the number of trained teachers and providing textbooks served by trained academic providers.
- ✓ It does not try to account for all factors that may be influencing operations and results as a conceptual framework would but instead focuses specifically on the project's activities and impacts.
  - ↓ The above is useful for programme managers and Monitoring and Evaluation planners as they clarify the direct relationships between elements of particular interest within a particular programme effort.
- ✓ It is important to understand that, within a programme, several activities can have their own inputs and outputs. Collectively, the outputs of the activities contribute to the programme outcomes and impacts.
- ✓ In some cases, the output of one programme activity could be an input for another activity. For example, if an activity is to develop guidelines, the output of that activity is the guidelines, which are an input in this overall logic model for quality education service delivery.

Different Monitoring And Evaluation Tools In The Logic Frameworks

Let us use the scenario of a school setting as a case study.

Input

- ✓ Financial resources.
- ✓ Textbook procurement.
- ✓ Personnel Recruitment.
- ✓ Training Planning.

Process

- ✓ Provide training for schoolteachers.
- ✓ Supply textbooks to secondary schools.
- ✓ Employ more teachers.

Outputs

- ✓ The teacher-to-student ratio has increased.
- ✓ Students get access to more books.
- ✓ More knowledgeable training and education.

Outcome

- ✓ Students increase their reading culture.
- ✓ Training content for students has improved.

Impact

- ✓ Students' result improves.
- ✓ Students' interest in reading improves compared to before.
- ✓ Students interact more and better with teachers.
- ✓ Monitoring tools can be developed to measure any of the stages of the logic framework.
- ✓ Every stage has its unit of measurement, for example, the number of students who passed the main external exams this year.
- ✓ Results can be used as a ratio to measure impacts. For example, the increased pass rate of students following the intervention.

Fig. 6:2: Evaluation Tools in Logic Framework

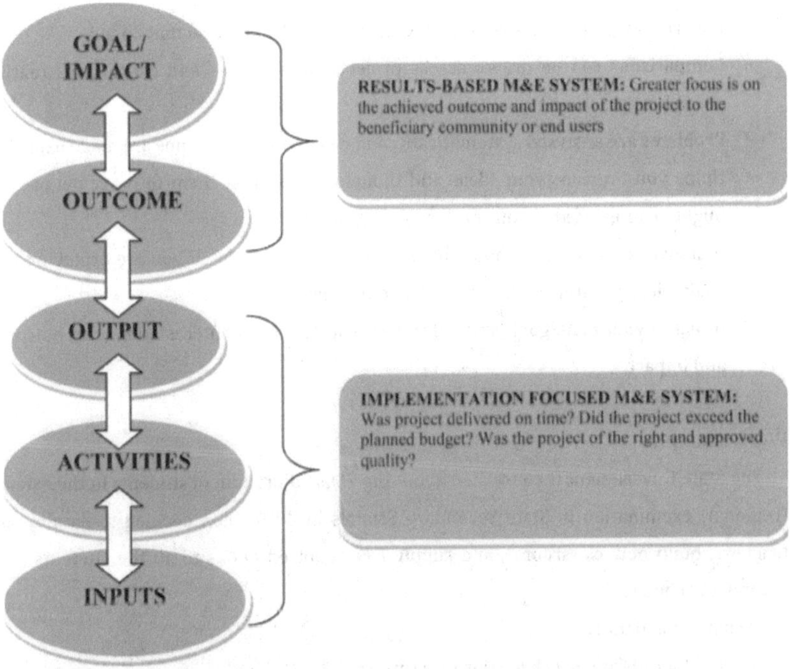

Image source: Academic Library

Pros & Cons Of Logical Framework

As a rule, donors and other public bodies prefer NGOs to report using metrics-based variables and indicators, particularly the logical framework.

Donors understandably have a concern over value for money and accountability. As such, the focus is on measurable empirical evidence, often in the form of numbers and quantifiable results, outputs, and outcomes.

Donors like the logical framework and metrics-based approaches for some of the clear advantages they bring.

Benefits: It ensures that:

- ✓ Objectives are clear, coherent, and measurable.
- ✓ Concrete evidence is sought for activities that work and those that do not.
- ✓ Comparisons can be drawn across projects/programmes and conclusions reached about best practices.
- ✓ Problems are analysed systematically, and risks and assumptions are made explicit.
- ✓ Helps you organise your ideas and thoughts to express them to other people who might be interested in your projects/ programme.
- ✓ It shows you what you should be measuring to determine if you are achieving your goals, clearly stating your outputs and outcomes.
- ✓ It makes your main goals and objectives clear to anyone interested in your outcomes and impact.

Work Examples

The State Government is concerned about the 75% failure rate of students in the external (regional) examination in State Secondary Schools in 2007, then decided to employ new teachers, build new classrooms, and supply free required books to all the students in its secondary schools.

Prepare and identify:

- ➤ The logical framework for this programme.
- ➤ Stages for Monitoring and Evaluation in the framework.
- ➤ Measurable indices in the framework.

If by 2011, the failure rate is 30%,

- ➤ What is the impact of the programme?
- ➤ Was the programme a success?

Activities: Design a project in the education or any sector of the economy you are familiar with, based on a specific objective to be targeted. Your project plan should contain/have the following:

✓ Identify one stage of each logic framework from the project.

✓ Describe the measurable indices of your project.

✓ What information can be given at each stage of the project?

✓ What is the outcome?

✓ Was the project impactful?

CHAPTER SEVEN (7) – EVALUATION PLAN

DESIGNING AN EVALUATION PLAN/MONITORING & EVALUATION SYSTEM

What Is A Monitoring And Evaluation System?

In development work, a Monitoring and Evaluation System represents all the things that need to be undertaken before, during, and after programme implementation, to track and measure progress (and success) in achieving the goal.

In other words, the Monitoring and Evaluation System would include things like:

- ✓ The person or people responsible for the Monitoring and Evaluation tasks in the organisation.
- ✓ The intervals where data should be collected.
- ✓ How is the data collected?
- ✓ Who collects the data?
- ✓ The type of database that is used for storing the data.
- ✓ The standard forms and data collection tools are to be used.
- ✓ How is the data analysed?
- ✓ The evaluation questions.
- ✓ The frequency with which an evaluation takes place.
- ✓ The budget allocated for evaluation, etc.

A more formal definition of a Monitoring and Evaluation System is a *"series of policies, practices and processes that enable the systematic and effective collection, analysis and use of Monitoring and Evaluation information."*

- Nigel Simister, October 2009.

Sometimes the terms 'Monitoring and Evaluation System' and 'Monitoring and Evaluation Plan' are used interchangeably. This is neither true nor correct. As explained in the opening paragraph of this chapter, "Monitoring and Evaluation System represents all the things that need to be undertaken before, during and after programme implementation, to track and measure progress (and success) in achieving the goal."

While an Evaluation Plan is part of the System, that is mostly concerned with the use of frameworks.

A review of the literature shows that there are many different ways and steps to develop a Monitoring and Evaluation System. There is not a best (or one) way to develop a Monitoring and Evaluation System. The system that is ultimately developed should fit your context, needs, and purposes.

With this said, though, a well-designed Monitoring and Evaluation System *"will ensure a consistent approach to the collection, analysis and use of information, whilst allowing considerable scope for different parts of an organisation to develop their own solutions in response to their own particular situations."*

- Tiina Pasanen and Louise Shaxson (2016).

Additionally, Monitoring and Evaluation Systems should ideally follow these guidelines or criteria,

    (i) relevance,

    (ii) coherence,

    (iii) effectiveness,

    (iv) efficiency,

    (v) impact and,

    (vi) sustainability.

These have been explained in an earlier chapter.

7 Steps For Setting Up A Monitoring & Evaluation System

Designing a Monitoring and Evaluation System is a complex task that usually involves staff from different units. This part of this chapter describes the development of such a system in 7 steps. Each step is linked with key questions, which are intended to stimulate a discussion of the current state of the Monitoring and Evaluation System in a project or an organisation. Therefore, the 7 steps do not represent a strict chronological sequence for the development of a Monitoring and Evaluation System. All steps should be considered from the beginning:

- **Step 1**: Define the purpose and scope of the Monitoring and Evaluation System.
- **Step 2**: Agree on outcomes and objectives - Theory of change (including indicators).
- **Step 3**: Plan data collection and analysis (including development of tools).
- **Step 4**: Plan the organisation of the data.
- **Step 5**: Plan the information flow and reporting requirements (how and for whom?).
- **Step 6**: Plan reflection processes and events.
- **Step 7**: Plan the necessary resources and skills.

Step 1: Define The Purpose And Scope Of The Monitoring And Evaluation System

It is crucial to define the scope of the Monitoring and Evaluation System at the very beginning. A question that will likely need to be answered is whether the system should be impact-oriented and whether we even want to monitor higher-level impacts, or whether the project team is satisfied with simply recording the proper implementation of activities and their results. Both can make sense and be correct, depending on the circumstances and what needs to be improved in the project in the best possible way. Of course, high-level results-oriented monitoring is usually preferable, but it could also fail due to the available capabilities. Moreover, it should be clear from the beginning who will continue to work with the Monitoring and Evaluation findings later on.

A challenge in this first step is engaging staff and convincing them that the additional time and effort to set up a Monitoring and Evaluation System is worthwhile to improve project steering and thus the quality of project or program results. There are many and varied activities that can be carried out to this end. For some project/programme teams, a workshop or a presentation may be helpful to convince them of the usefulness of monitoring; in other cases, various face-to-face discussions may be more appropriate. The approach must ultimately be decided by the person responsible for Monitoring and

Evaluation and depends on the resources available and the key people involved. Prior consultation on these can be useful.

Step 2: Agree On Outcomes And Objectives, Theory Of Change (Including Indicators)

A Theory of Change (ToC) is a description of how and why activities are expected to lead to short-, medium-, and long-term outcomes over a period of time. This is more than just identifying outcomes and objectives. A ToC is a set of impact assumptions or hypotheses that can be described as a visual diagram, a narrative, or both. Once there is a ToC or something similar, staff will know better which Monitoring and Evaluation data to collect.

ToCs are not necessarily complex, but they do provide a way to summarise the complexity of a situation and bring clarity to it. At best, this allows a wide range of stakeholders to come to a shared understanding of why and how activities will lead to desired results.

It is helpful to involve a variety of stakeholders when developing the ToC – this could include staff, beneficiaries, partners, funders, and even other experts who are familiar with the technical theme. The development process and the thinking involved are often as important as the diagram or narrative produced.

However, if this seems too time-consuming, a common and good practice is to produce a first draft, which can then be discussed with other key stakeholders. The result of this work should be a complete but not over-complicated description of the activities and their results, with prioritised outcomes for measurement and SMART indicators to collect data against them.

Of course, ToCs need regular review because as context and needs change, so do they. However, high-level outcomes and impacts are usually valid for some years.

It is worth noting that an important critique of ToC is that it neglects social realities and possible negative project effects, and that it might narrow the view on planned project/program goals.

Step 3: Plan Data Collection And Analysis (Including Development Of Tools)

For this step, it is recommended to create a Monitoring and Evaluation work plan, a Monitoring and Evaluation matrix, or a combination of both. Depending on the needs of a program or project, the design of such a document may vary greatly. However, to ensure that the Monitoring and Evaluation activities are implemented, it is advisable to determine in such a matrix clear responsibility with timelines or frequencies of data collection.

The methods to collect the data depend on the information needed. For example, if quantitative information on jobs created is needed, then a survey with a standardised questionnaire may be useful, whereas if information on the reasons for behavioural changes of supported groups is required, qualitative interviews or a combination of interviews and a standardised survey may be more useful. Data collection tools (for example, interview guidelines and questionnaires) should be pre-tested before they are used. Important guidance on how to develop such tools can also be found in the aforementioned Evaluation Toolbox and on the websites of INTRAC. Some of the staff involved probably need to have analytical skills (for example, statistical skills in the case of the analysis of questionnaires). If such skills are missing or there is no time to develop the required tools or to analyse the collected data, hiring an external Monitoring and Evaluation expert could be considered.

For some programs or projects, there might be a Monitoring and Evaluation officer who coordinates such Monitoring and Evaluation activities. If this is not the case, then it will be necessary for the staff to coordinate the activities among themselves. It will then be even more important to assign clear responsibilities within the team.

Are you trying to decide whether to build an internal tool, work with external contractors, or use an off-the-shelf tool?

Step 4: Plan The Organisation Of The Data

To use the collected data, the information needs to be stored and shared with the people involved, regardless of their location. One can store data physically or digitally using an information system. This means that Monitoring and Evaluation systems and data management go together. The data management system should be designed according to the needs, size, and complexity of the project or program. Staff engaged in Monitoring and Evaluation activities may need to liaise with the IT support of their organisation. In any case, it is important to label and organise items in storage clearly (chronological, by location, by content, or any other category considered useful).

Good data management includes storing data securely to avoid unauthorised access, theft, or unintentional destruction of data and to comply with any legal requirements, such as data protection legislation. This often involves IT protection methods, such as passwords, firewalls, and virus checks. But it might also simply mean having a lock on a filing cabinet. The global collaboration organisation *Better Evaluation synthesizing advice from the UK Data Archive* recommends: not storing digital data on externally networked servers or computers; the installation of firewalls and security systems to protect against malware and viruses; the existence of password-protected computer systems; the encryption of sensitive materials (even when transferring data by email); the signing of non-disclosure agreements. If a survey needs to include personal data, such as address or name, it is essential to obtain the permission of the respondent beforehand.

When using external software for data management needs, the terms of use, data protection and confidentiality, and the servers' location should be checked.

Data management is linked with data quality assurance, too: It is important to avoid gathering data of low quality and to ensure that data is "cleaned" of any errors. The collected data may be the basis for further decisions. Data quality methods may include the use of multiple data sources, such as triangulation of data and interviewer training and supervision. It should be clarified among the staff who is responsible for data quality assurance and how.

Step 5: Plan The Information Flow And Reporting Requirements (How And For Whom?)

To be useful, information gained through Monitoring and Evaluation needs to be communicated to different stakeholders. Most likely, there are certain reporting requirements set by donors. However, it is good practice to disseminate and discuss findings among other stakeholder groups so that learning from Monitoring and Evaluation has a wider reach. At the very least, the Monitoring and Evaluation results should also be discussed with the supported communities and groups.

There are many ways to communicate Monitoring and Evaluation information with stakeholder groups. The best communication method will depend on the audience and how the information will be used. For example, project managers may require much more detailed information on the progress made; program directors may require regular, summary reports across different projects and programs, with aggregated tables and statistics; policy-makers might benefit from a short brief summarizing the main issues, and making recommendations for change; a member of the public that supports an organization through donations might prefer to see a story of change, a photograph or a short video that enables to connect with beneficiaries on an emotional level.

Sometimes, especially when communicating information to partners or supported groups, it is useful to discuss communication methods with the audience beforehand. This is a core element of participatory Monitoring and Evaluation. Consideration should also be given to how information can be communicated to people with audio or visual disabilities, or whether stakeholders can access the venues for meetings. When communicating information to illiterate or semi-literate people, presenting information in written form is of little use.

It is also important to know when information needs to be communicated. For example, if decision-making meetings occur quarterly, then it is important to communicate the Monitoring and Evaluation findings before those meetings are held. Similarly, when seeking to influence a government policy, it is important to supply information at the right time so that it has the maximum chance of achieving its purpose.

The use of communication strategies or dissemination plans will facilitate the organisation of the information flow. The key point is to be very clear about who needs what Monitoring and Evaluation information, when, and where. Narratives (formal reports, case studies, newsletters, press releases, policy briefs) are the most common way of communicating Monitoring and Evaluation findings. Other means of communication are through photographs, videos, pictures, and cartoons. The big advantage of the latter-mentioned communication channels is that they can communicate information from supported communities and groups directly to different audiences, without being filtered through a report. In addition, Monitoring and Evaluation findings can be communicated verbally in meetings and workshops, through feedback sessions, and even through informal conversations. Speaking directly to a target audience allows messages to be tailored to the individual or group and allows for some discussion of findings as well.

Also, more artistic and traditional methods of communication, such as poems, drama, mime, and song, can be used to share Monitoring and Evaluation information with others. Using such activities can help prevent Monitoring and Evaluation from becoming a sterile exercise and can foster a broader understanding and discussions about change.

Recent technological advances offer another way of communicating Monitoring and Evaluation information. Websites and social media sites, podcasting, and webinars have made it much easier to present and communicate information in new and innovative ways. Communication via mobile phones and tablets offers further opportunities in the communication of Monitoring and Evaluation information, although to date, this has mainly been used for data collection (for example, surveying through text messages) rather than for communication of Monitoring and Evaluation findings.

The dissemination plan below provides a good example of what such a plan could look like.

Dissemination Plan				
Audience	Purpose	Message	Products and channels	Timeline
Who do you want to reach, who needs to learn about your experience?	*For each target audience: what is the purpose of sharing with them?*	*For each target audience: what are the lessons that you want to share with them?*	*For each target audience: what are the best ways to reach them?*	*For each product/ channel: when do you plan to share? Which steps need to be taken?*
1.				
2.				
Etc...				

Source: Website of the CTA. Technical Centre for Agricultural and Rural Cooperation, licensed under a Creative Commons Attribution-Share Alike 3.0 Unported License.

In some organisations, there is a communications officer responsible for external communications and organising the flow of information; in others, especially smaller organisations, this task is the responsibility of a Monitoring and Evaluation officer or the project team itself.

Step 6: Plan Reflection Processes And Events

This step goes a bit further and wants to not only communicate results but also discuss Monitoring and Evaluation findings with stakeholders so that everyone learns from each other. Again, the discussion and learning formats can vary widely. These could include workshops, exchange visits, seminars, conferences, and After-Action Reviews (AAR), to name a few. However, learning does not happen in one sitting. Moments of reflection must take place regularly throughout the life of the project or program. The incorporation of learning events in the project/program cycle is key. In this regard, annual or bi-annual reviews are critical learning opportunities to reach conclusions about achievements and failures. The optimal sequence of learning events follows reporting lines of decision-making. It should be ensured that the right people are involved in such reviews. Therefore, it may sometimes be important to include decision-makers in the reviews (so that they learn at the same time as their staff and therefore make appropriate decisions), but it can be a challenge to ensure that this does not affect the openness of the conversations. It could be very helpful if staff were trained in facilitating intentional group learning processes.

Regular team meetings are another important opportunity for reflection. Team members may include project staff, implementing partners, and primary stakeholder representatives – this depends on how the project is structured. Weekly meetings are common, but if other stakeholders are involved, this may be needed less frequently. In each project context, there are usually forums where implementing partners interact with each other. These events offer another chance for reflection.

It is recommended to assign roles and responsibilities for leading the learning events. In addition, the learning and resulting conclusions for further actions should be documented well, with a focus on documenting "action needed", "person responsible for implementation", "deadline", and "persons responsible for follow-up". Such documentation could be tabular (see the example below), but any other form is fine as long as it records the most important items.

Documenting learning and conclusions

Weakness identified	Improved action suggested	Person(s) responsible for action	Timel for ine	Unit/person responsible for follow-ups

Lastly, it is worth mentioning here that learning in the context of Monitoring and Evaluation is about having a culture that encourages intentional reflection and processes that support this culture. All teams learn as they implement project activities. But to take advantage of this learning and consistently translate it into improved practice, learning must be planned and managed.

Step 7: Plan The Necessary Resources And Skills

It is good to start planning the Monitoring and Evaluation budget already in the project/program design phase so that adequate funds are allocated and later available for Monitoring and Evaluation activities. There is no standard formula to determine the budget for a project/programme's Monitoring and Evaluation System. An industry standard is that between 3 and 10 per cent of a project/programme's budget should be allocated to Monitoring and Evaluation. A planning table for key Monitoring and Evaluation activities can be useful in this regard. It is particularly important to budget for any expensive items, such as baseline surveys and evaluations.

Moreover, an effective Monitoring and Evaluation system requires capable people. Therefore, when defining roles and responsibilities for Monitoring and Evaluation, specific consideration should be given to the Monitoring and Evaluation qualifications and expectations, including the approximate proportion of time for each person to support the system. The first step in planning for the Monitoring and Evaluation of human resources is to determine the available Monitoring and Evaluation experience within the project/program team, partner organisations, target communities, and any other potential participants in the Monitoring and Evaluation System. This will inform the need for capacity building or outside expertise. For long-term and larger projects/programs, it may be useful to create a Monitoring and Evaluation training schedule. Ideally, data collection, analysis, and Monitoring and Evaluation training involve the people to whom these processes and decisions most relate.

One key planning consideration is who will have the overall responsibility for the Monitoring and Evaluation System. It is important to identify who will coordinate all these Monitoring and Evaluation activities and to whom others will turn for Monitoring and Evaluation guidance. The responsible person or team should supervise the Monitoring and Evaluation functions and have an overview of any problems that might arise.

This article was written to support especially smaller organisations in their Monitoring and Evaluation activities. Hopefully, the information has been helpful and of practical use in setting up Monitoring and Evaluation Systems. The author welcomes suggestions, additions, and comments.

How To Write A Monitoring And Evaluation Framework

A **Monitoring and Evaluation** framework is *one part* of a **Monitoring and Evaluation** plan, which describes how the whole **Monitoring and Evaluation** system for the program or organisation works. A **Monitoring and Evaluation** framework can also be called an evaluation matrix.

A **Monitoring and Evaluation** framework is one part of a **Monitoring and Evaluation** plan, which describes how the whole Monitoring and Evaluation System for the program or organisation works.

Choose Your Indicators

The first step in writing a Monitoring and Evaluation framework is to decide which indicators you will use to measure the success of your program. This is a very important step, so you should try to involve as many people as possible to get different perspectives.

You need to choose indicators for each level of your programme – outputs, outcomes, and goals. There can be more than one indicator for each level, although you should try to keep the total number of indicators manageable.

Each indicator should be:

- Directly related to the output, outcome, or goal listed on the problem tree or log frame.

- Something that you can measure accurately using either qualitative or quantitative methods, and your available resources.

- If possible, a standard indicator that is commonly used for this type of program. For example, poverty could be measured using the Progress Out of Poverty Index. Using standard indicators can be better because they are already well-defined, there are tools available to measure them, and you will be able to compare your results to other programs or national statistics.

Here is an example of some indicators for the goal, outcome and output of an education program:

Goal

10% increase in the number of Grades 6 primary students continuing on to high school within 3 years

Indicator

Percentage of Grades 5-6 primary students continuing on to high school

Outcome

Improve reading proficiency among children in Grades 5-6 by 20% within 3 years

Average reading proficiency among children in Grades 5-6

Output

1. 500 Grade 5-6 students with low reading proficiency complete a reading summer camp

Number of students completing the reading summer camp

Some organisations have very strict rules about how the indicators must be written (for example, they must always start with a number or must always contain an adjective). It is advised that these rules usually lead to indicators that are convoluted or don't make sense. It is advised to make sure the indicators are written in a way that everyone involved in the project (including the donor) can understand them.

Define Each Indicator

Once you have chosen your indicators, you need to write a definition for each one. The definition describes *exactly* how the indicator is calculated. If you do not have definitions, there is a serious risk that indicators might be calculated differently at different times, which means the results cannot be compared.

Here is an example of how one indicator in the education program is defined:

Indicator

Percentage of Grades 6 primary students continuing on to high school.

Definition

Number students who start the first day of Grade 7 divided by the total number of Grade 6 students in the previous year, multiplied by 100.

Sample calculation

$$\frac{80 \text{ students start the first day of Grade 7 in 2013}}{175 \text{ Grade 6 students in 2012}} \times 100 = 46\%$$

After writing the definition of each indicator, you also need to identify where the data will come from (the "data source"). Common sources are baseline and end-line surveys, monitoring reports, and existing information systems. You also need to decide how frequently it will be measured (monthly, quarterly, annually, etc.).

Measure The Baseline And Set The Target

Before you start your programme, you need to measure the starting value of each indicator – this is called the "baseline". In the education example above, that means you would need to measure the current percentage of Grade 6 students continuing to Grade 7 (before you start your program).

In some cases, you will need to survey to measure the baseline. In other cases, you might have existing data available. In this case, you need to make sure the existing data is using the same definition as you for calculating the indicator.

Once you know the baseline, you need to set a target for improvement. Before you set the target, it's important to do some research on what a realistic target is. Many people set unachievable targets, without realising it. For example, someone once worked on a project where the target was a 25% reduction in the child mortality rate within 12 months. However, a brief review of other child health programs showed that even the best programs only managed a 10-20% reduction within 5 years.

Identify Who Is Responsible And Where The Results Will Be Reported

The final step is to decide who will be responsible for measuring each indicator. Output indicators are often measured by field staff or program managers, while outcome and goal indicators may be measured by evaluation consultants or even national agencies.

You also need to decide where the results for each indicator will be reported. This could be in your monthly program reports, annual donor reports, or on your website. Indicator results are used to assess whether the program is working or not, so decision-makers and stakeholders (not just the donor) must have access to them as soon as possible.

Put It All Into The Template

Once you have completed all these steps, you are now ready to put everything into the Monitoring and Evaluation framework template.

NB: You can find a very easy-to-use and useful template from this link: https://tools4dev.org/resources/me-framework-template/

References (for this chapter):

https://www.activityinfo.org/blog/posts/2022-01-06-seven-steps-for-setting-up-a-monitoring-and-evaluation-system.html

https://www.annmurraybrown.com/single-post/2016/04/01/how-to-design-a-monitoring-and-evaluation-me-system

https://tools4dev.org/resources/monitoring-evaluation-plan-template/

CHAPTER EIGHT (8) – ACTION RESEARCH

INTRODUCTION: Action Research is one of those terms that we hear quite often in today's educational circles.

Typically, Action Research is undertaken in a school setting. It is a reflective process that allows for inquiry and discussion as components of the "research." Often, Action Research is a collaborative activity among colleagues searching for solutions to everyday, real problems experienced in schools, or looking for ways to improve instruction and increase student achievement. Rather than dealing with the theoretical, Action Research allows practitioners to address those concerns that are closest to them, ones over which they can exert some influence and make necessary adjustments and changes.

Practitioners are responsible for making more and more decisions in the operations of schools, and they are being held publicly accountable for students' achievements and results. The process of Action Research assists educators in assessing needs, documenting the steps of inquiry, analysing data, and making informed decisions that can lead to desired outcomes.

What is Action Research?

Action Research is a process in which participants examine their own educational practice(s) systematically and carefully, using the techniques of research. It is based on the following assumptions:

- ✓ Teachers and principals work best on problems they have identified for themselves.
- ✓ Teachers and principals become more effective when encouraged to examine and assess their own work and then consider ways of working differently.
- ✓ Teachers and principals help each other by working collaboratively.
- ✓ Working with colleagues helps teachers and principals in their professional development.

What Action Research Is Not

Action Research is not what usually comes to mind when we hear the word "research." Action Research is not a library project where we learn more about a topic that interests us. It is not problem-solving in the sense of trying to find out what is wrong, but rather a quest for knowledge about how to improve. Action Research is not about doing research on or about people or finding all available information on a topic, but about looking for the correct Action Research.

Types Of Action Research

Individual Teacher Research usually focuses on a single issue in the classroom. The teacher may be seeking solutions to problems of classroom management, instructional strategies, use of materials, student learning, tests, and evaluations, etc. Teachers may have the support of their supervisor or principal, an instructor for a course they are taking, or parents. The problem is one that the teacher believes is evident in his or her classroom, and one that can be addressed on an individual basis. The research may then be such that the teacher collects data or may involve looking at student participation. One of the drawbacks of individual research is that it may not be shared with others unless the teacher chooses to present findings at a faculty meeting, make a formal presentation at a conference, or submit written material.

Several teachers could be working concurrently on the same problem with no knowledge of the work of others, which is one of the challenges of this type of Action Research.

Collaborative Action Research may include as few as two teachers or a group of several teachers and others interested in addressing a classroom or department issue. This issue may involve one classroom or a common problem shared by many classrooms. These teachers may be supported by individuals outside of the school, such as a university or community partner.

School-wide research focuses on issues common to all. For example, a school may have a concern about the lack of parental involvement in activities and is looking for a way to reach more parents to involve them in meaningful ways.

Or the school may be looking to address its organisational and decision-making structures. Teams of staff from the school may work together to narrow the question, gather, and analyse the data, and decide on a plan of action.

An example of Action Research for a school could be to examine their state test scores to identify areas that need improvement and then determine a plan of action to improve student performance.

District-wide research is far more complex and utilises more resources, but the rewards can be great. Issues can be organisational, community-based, performance-based, or processes for decision-making. A district may choose to address a problem common to several schools or one of organisational management.

Downsides are the documentation requirements (communication) to keep everyone in the loop, and the ability to keep the process in motion. Collecting data from all participants needs a commitment from staff to do their fair share and to meet agreed-upon deadlines for assignments.

On the positive side, real school reform and change can take hold based on a common understanding through inquiry. The involvement of multiple constituent groups can lend energy to the process and create an environment of genuine stakeholders.

Steps In Action Research

Within all the definitions of Action Research, there are four basic themes:

1) Empowerment of participants,
2) Collaboration through participation,
3) Acquisition of knowledge, and
4) Social change.

In conducting Action Research, we structure routines for continuous confrontation with data on the health of a school community. These routines are loosely guided by movement through five phases of inquiry:

Fig. 8.1: Steps in Action Research

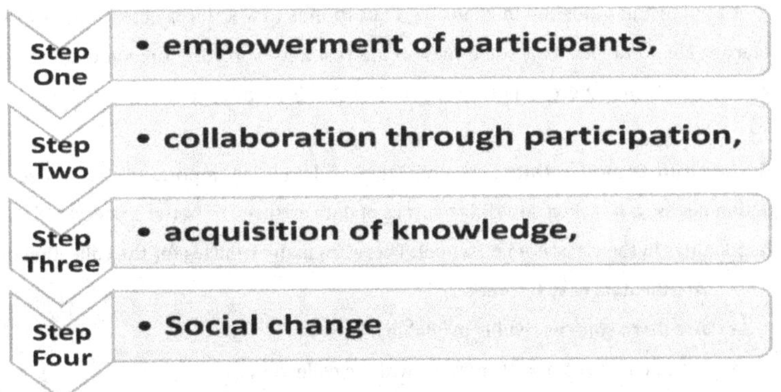

Fig. 8.2: Action Research Cycle

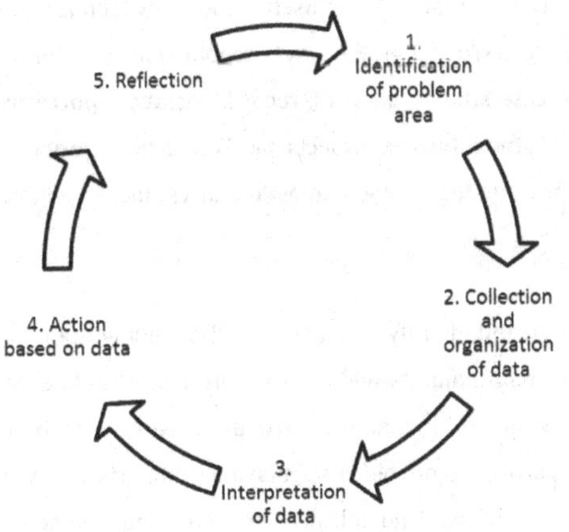

Identify A Problem Area: Teachers often have several questions they wish to investigate. However, it is important to limit the question to one that is meaningful and doable in the confines of their daily work. Careful planning at this first stage will limit false starts and frustrations. There are several criteria to consider before investing the time and effort in "researching" a problem.

An important guideline in choosing a question is to ask if it is something over which the teacher has influence. Is it something of interest and worth the time and effort that will be spent? Sometimes there is a discrete problem that is readily identifiable.

Gather And Organise Data: The collection of data is an important step in deciding what action needs to be taken. Multiple sources of data are used to better understand the scope of happenings in the classroom or school. There are many vehicles for the collection of data.

- ✓ Are the data easy to collect?
- ✓ Are there sources readily available for use?
- ✓ How structured and systematic will the collection be?

NB: Use at least three sources (triangulation) of data for the basis of actions.

Organise the data in a way that makes it useful to identify trends and themes. Data can be arranged by; gender, classroom, grade level, school, journals, individual files, logs of meetings, videotapes, case studies, surveys, records – tests, report cards, attendance, self-assessment, samples of student work, projects, performances, interviews, portfolios, diaries, field notes, audio tapes, photos, memos, questionnaires, focus groups, anecdotal records, checklists, etc.

Interpret Data: Analyse and identify major themes. Depending upon the question, teachers may wish to use classroom data, individual data, or subgroup data. Some of the data are quantifiable and can be analysed without the use of statistics or technical assistance. Other data, such as opinions, attitudes, or checklists, may be summarised in table form. Data that is not quantifiable can be reviewed holistically, and important elements or themes can be noted.

Act On Evidence: Using the information from the data collection and review of current literature, design a plan of action that will allow you to make a change and study that change. Only one variable must be altered. As with any experiment, if several changes are made at once, it will be difficult to determine which action is responsible for the outcome. While the new technique is being implemented, continue to document and collect data on performance.

Evaluate Results: Assess the effects of the intervention to determine if improvement has occurred. If there is improvement, do the data provide the supporting evidence? If no, what changes can be made to the actions to elicit better results?

Next Step(s): As a result of the Action Research project, identify additional questions raised by the data and plan for additional improvements, revisions, and next steps.

Repeat steps again and again and again!!!

Benefits Of Action Research
- ✓ It allows teachers to learn.
- ✓ Help to confer relevance and validity to a disciplined study.
- ✓ Focus on school issues, problems, or areas of collective interest.
- ✓ It is also a form of teacher professional development.
- ✓ Collegial interactions: isolation is one of the downsides of teaching.
- ✓ Teachers are more apt to look at questions that address the school rather than questions that affect the individual teacher.
- ✓ Reflect on your practice.
- ✓ Improved communication

Fig. 8.3: Action Research Design

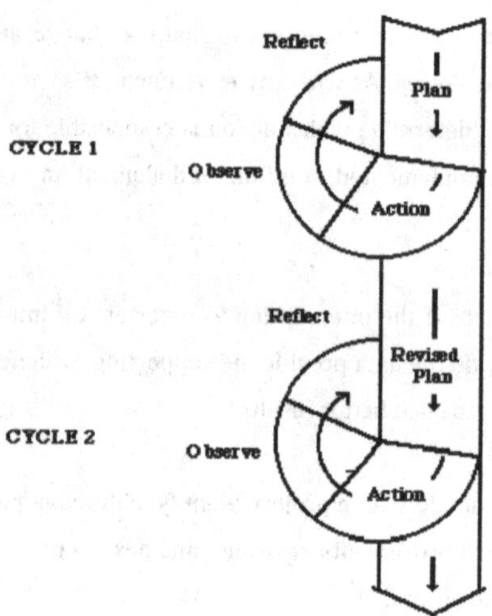

Action Research Application: Objectives of a standard school include, but are not limited to:

- ✓ Ensure that pupil/student is taught, and learns – all round: communication and language, physical development, personal, social, and emotional development.
- ✓ Ensure that studying and learning take place.
- ✓ Ensure that proper education and learning are paramount and preeminent.
- ✓ Ensure and encourage discipline (everywhere).
- ✓ Encourage social/communal responsibility.

Activities:

Who are the players in the Educational Sector?

- ✓ Students,
- ✓ Teachers, and

✓ Coordinators.

What are the roles/duties of these players?

✓ Students

✓ Teachers

✓ Coordinators

What are the factors that hinder you as a teacher from achieving the objectives of Action Research?

CHAPTER NINE (9) – DATA AND DATA COLLECTION

As an evaluator, all the aspects of this handbook are useful and necessary because of the importance of evaluation. But I will particularly encourage you to pay special attention to this chapter and the next few chapters, as these chapters will be dealing with what can easily, and can arguably be considered to be the most important aspect of Monitoring and Evaluation, because if we get this aspect of the evaluation exercise wrong, then we would not have conducted anything seriously meaningful, or/and we would come out with misleading evaluation results, conclusion, leading to wrong and erroneous suggestions and recommendations that could hurt the organisation and other users of the evaluation, and that aspect of the evaluation exercise we would be looking at is; **DATA**.

Data Versus Information

Information is defined as knowledge; definite knowledge acquired or supplied about something or somebody. *A bulletin giving the latest information on the trial*, gathering facts, the collected facts, and data about a specific subject.

Data is defined as factual information; information, often in the form of facts or figures obtained from experiments and surveys, used as a basis for making calculations or drawing conclusions.

Source: Microsoft® Encarta® Microsoft Corporation.

Take a look at the two (2) sentences/statements below;
- ✓ There is a bridge ahead. (Information).
- ✓ There is a narrow bridge approximately 50m ahead! (Data).

In essence, processes and evaluation exercises are not meant to provide information, but data (facts and figures) obtained from proper and deliberate exercise(s), that is, the evaluation processes, and used as a basis for making and drawing conclusions for planning.

Data Collection: Data collection helps your team assess the health of your process. To do so, you must identify the key quality characteristics you will measure, how you will measure them, and what you will do with the data you collect.

Key quality characteristics are those factors your client/project owners or sponsors deem as important to them, usually enumerated in the objectives or Terms of Reference (ToR).

> Simply collecting data does not ensure that you will obtain relevant or specific enough data to tell you what is occurring in your process. The key issue is not "*How do we collect data?*" Rather, it is: *How do we obtain useful data?*

Fig. 9.1: Differences/Similarities Between Information & Data

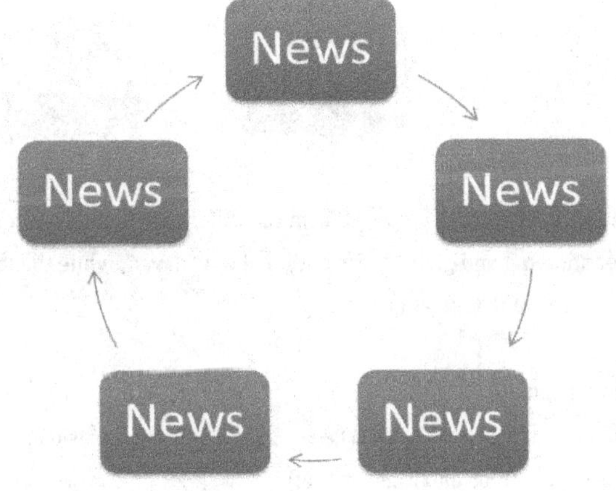

Fig. 9.2: Differences/Similarities Between Information & Data

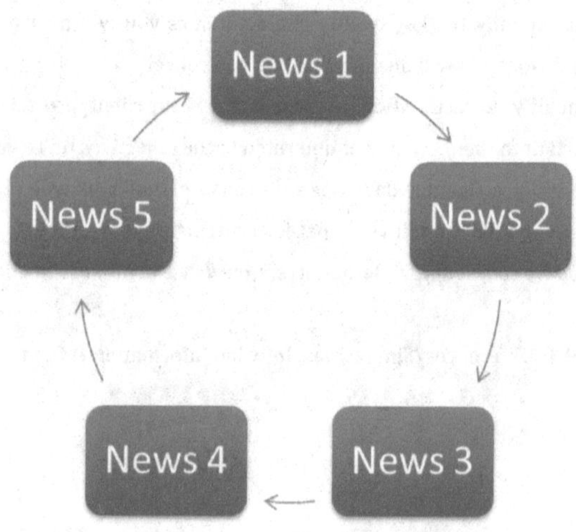

Fig. 9.1 and Fig. 9.2 depict in pictorial form the difference between information and data, with the former showing and giving information about "news", while the latter shows which news item comes first and in what order.

Data Collection; Types:

Data types are either QUANTITATIVE (by counting/measuring) or QUALITATIVE (by observing, asking, and interpreting).

Data are also primary and secondary.

Basic Data Types:

✓ Baseline data.

✓ Project field records.

✓ Qualitative Data (quality): These types of data can only be observed, but not measured (it *describes* something), for example, "*conducive learning environment*", "a brilliant student", or "a big school compound".

✓ Quantitative Data (quantity): These types of data are numerical information (numbers), which can either be discrete or continuous. For example, the number of students in a class and the weight of each student in a class.

Quantitative Data

Discrete Data: This can only take certain/definite values (like whole numbers). For example, 5, 19, 24, 979

Continuous Data: This can take any value (within a range). For example, 3.53, 7.80, 56.9

Note: *Discrete data is counted, and Continuous data is measured*

Data Collection; Types:

Primary Data: Primary data is data that is collected directly through the use of surveys, meetings, focus group discussions, interviews, or other methods that involve direct contact with the respondents – women, men, boys, and girls, for a particular purpose for which it is collected.

Secondary Data: By contrast, secondary data is existing data that has been, or will be, collected by others for another or other purposes, other than for which it was originally collected. Secondary data may include mapping data, data from the mid-term or final evaluation of a previous phase of operations, data collected by other organisations, or the district concerned, or data gathered by research organisations.

Routine data collected by institutions participating in an activity (for example, schools and health centres) are exceptionally good sources of secondary data which cannot be replicated by primary data collection without prohibitive expense.

Distinction Between Primary and Secondary Data

The critical distinction between the two (2) types of data is that primary data is collected by someone who has been hired specifically for the purpose for which the data are required.

Secondary data have been, or will be, collected for another primary purpose. For example, all secondary data were or are primary data for another study but may be used for "secondary" purposes related to Monitoring and Evaluation in other projects.

Data Collection Methods: The following are some of the data collection methods that are available:

- ✓ Observation.
- ✓ Surveys (Research, Sampling, Polls).
- ✓ Questionnaires.
- ✓ Appraisals.
- ✓ Interviews.
- ✓ Participatory.
- ✓ Emotive.
- ✓ Frameworks (Templates).

Data Collection Procedures: Your evaluation process needs a well-defined data collection plan to:

- ✓ Point of data to be collected (place and time).
- ✓ Data are standardised, consistent, and uniform. So, it becomes easy to analyse.

The elements and objectives of data are clearly defined during the collection plan. This is where you also determine:

- ✓ What exactly do you need?
- ✓ Who will collect the data?
- ✓ What data to collect or leave out?
- ✓ Unit(s) of measurement?
- ✓ How to collect data (sampling, whole, etc)?
- ✓ Frequency of/for data collection?

Importance and Essence of Data

- ✓ To establish a factual/scientific basis for making decisions.
- ✓ To check for improvement against baseline information.
- ✓ For planning.

I think the problem is . . ., becomes. *The data indicates the problem is . . .*

Data Collection: Useful Data

Data collection helps your team assess the health of your process. To do so, you must identify the key quality characteristics you will measure, how you will measure them, and what you will do with the data you collect.

NB: The issue is not: *How do we collect data?* It is: *How do we obtain useful data?*

Attributes of Useful and Good Data include (but are not limited to):

- ✓ Accuracy,
- ✓ Promptness,
- ✓ Relevance/Significance,
- ✓ Agreed procedures used and followed,
- ✓ Etc.

Attributes of data to be collected should be determined by project/programme objectives.

Activities

- ✓ List ten (10) qualitative data that can be collected by your organisation.
- ✓ List ten (10) quantitative data that can be collected by your organisation.
- ✓ Your school/district needs to improve the pass rate in Mathematics; what data is needed?
- ✓ Design a data collection plan.
- ✓ List five (5) sources of secondary data for school administrators.

CHAPTER TEN (10) – DATA ANALYSIS

Data Analysis: Data analysis is a practice in which raw data is ordered, organised, and modelled scientifically (not guesswork) so that useful information can be extracted from it, which can be used in suggesting conclusions or supporting decisions.

In the course of analysing the data, trends or patterns often emerge, which should be highlighted in a report, preferably diagrammatically (visualisation), to capture the attention of the reader, and for ease of understanding, as everyone generally understands pictures and images.

Data interpretation entails explaining those trends or patterns.

Importance of Data Analysis

- ✓ To explain cause-and-effect phenomena.
- ✓ To relate findings to real-world events.
- ✓ To predict/forecast real-world phenomena based on findings.
- ✓ Finding answers to a particular problem.
- ✓ Making conclusions about real-world events based on the problem.
- ✓ Learning a lesson from the problem.

Since data "cannot talk" without analysis, analysing data will enable one to do the following:

- ✓ Interpret,
- ✓ Evaluate,
- ✓ Illustrate,
- ✓ Discuss,
- ✓ Explain,
- ✓ Clarify,
- ✓ Compare, and
- ✓ Contrast.

Data Analysis Planning

- ✓ Think about analysis early, as early as the initial planning stage of the evaluation exercise.
- ✓ Start with a plan.
- ✓ Code and enter data.
- ✓ Analyse.
- ✓ Interpret, and
- ✓ Reflect. When we reflect, we can achieve the following:
  - What did we learn?
  - What conclusions can we draw?
  - What are our recommendations?
  - What are the limitations of our analysis?

Why Do I Need An Analysis Plan?

- ✓ Make sure the questions and your data collection instrument get the information you want.
- ✓ Think about your "report" when you are designing your data collection instruments.

Qualitative Or Quantitative Approach?

Depending on the kind of data collected, the depth of knowledge desired, and the number of participants involved. Data analysis can either be qualitative or quantitative.

For Qualitative data, Qualitative data analysis applies.

For Quantitative data, Quantitative data analysis applies.

Quantitative Data Analysis

- ✓ Used for presenting and interpreting numerical data.
- ✓ Involves the use of descriptive statistical analysis tools like mean, median, mode, standard deviation, range, cumulative frequency, etc.
- ✓ The outcome is deductive.
- ✓ Sample surveys and structured interviews are mostly used in data collection, and a large amount of data is usually collected.

✓ Since it collects data on more participants, it is not possible to have the depth and breadth of knowledge about each.

✓ It is objective.

✓ Characteristics of the data may be described and explored by drawing graphs and charts and doing cross-tabulations – visualisation.

Quantitative Data Analysis Method

✓ Descriptive Statistics - for the absolute representation of data.

✓ Graphical Analysis – Bar charts, pie charts, and line graphs.

✓ Frequency Table.

✓ Cross Tabulation.

Descriptive Statistics (*Quantitative Data Analysis*)

✓ Ratio.

✓ Percentage.

✓ Frequency Table – Histogram, Frequency polygon, cumulative frequency curve.

✓ Percentile Curve.

✓ Line Graphic.

✓ Central Tendency – mean, median, mode, standard deviation, variance, etc.

Qualitative Data Analysis

✓ Seeks to explore attitudes, behaviours, and experiences.

✓ Focuses on differences in quality and results are in words or pictures rather than numbers.

✓ Usually have fewer participants.

✓ Provides a depth and richness of data not possible with quantitative data.

✓ The outcome is inductive.

✓ Observation, interview, focus group, and discussions, open-ended questions, and questionnaires are mostly used in data collection.

✓ It is subjective.

✓ Create insights about situations or problems where we would like to have more knowledge.

Qualitative Data Analysis Methods

Qualitative data analysis describes and summarises the mass of words generated by interviews or observational data through the following methods:

✓ **Thematic Analysis**: It emphasises identifying, analysing, and interpreting patterns of meaning within qualitative data.

✓ **Comparative Analysis**: Qualitative comparative analysis (QCA) is a set-based theory that seeks to explain the relationship between causal conditions and outcomes through the concept of sets and their relations. QCA models causal conditions as a superset or subset of relationships between an outcome and explanatory factors.

✓ **Content Analysis**: Involves a process designed to condense raw data into categories or themes based on valid inference and interpretation. This process uses inductive reasoning, by which themes and categories emerge from the data through the researcher's careful examination and constant comparison.

✓ **Discourse Analysis**: The Oxford English Dictionary defines discourse analysis as: "Linguistics, a method of analysing the structure of texts or utterances longer than one sentence, taking into account both their linguistic content and their sociolinguistic context; analysis performed using this method." Discourse analysis is a qualitative and interpretive method of analysing texts (in contrast to more systematic methods like content analysis). You make interpretations based on both the details of the material itself and on contextual knowledge.

✓ **Grounded Theory**: It is a research method concerned with the generation of theory 1, which is 'grounded' in data that has been systematically collected and analysed, and 2, it is used to uncover such things as social relationships and behaviours of groups, known as social processes. For example, attempts to unravel the meanings of people's interactions, social actions, and experiences. In other words, these explanations are grounded in the participants' own interpretations or explanations.

Content Analysis (*Qualitative Data Analysis*)

1. Read transcripts of interviews and discussions, or observations recorded.
2. Highlight key quotes/answers.
3. Code quotes/answers.
4. Sort quotes into coded groups/categories (themes).
5. Display summaries of data in such a way that interpretation becomes easy. For example, by preparing compilation sheets, flowcharts, diagrams, or matrices.
6. Interpret data patterns and conclude.

Data Analysis Guidelines

When analysing:

- ✓ Be objective.
- ✓ Accurate.
- ✓ True.
- ✓ Separate facts from opinions.
- ✓ Avoid "wrong" reasoning/argument. For example, mistakes in interpretation.

CHAPTER ELEVEN (11) – ANALYSIS TOOL

DATA ANALYSIS TOOLS (APPLICATIONS) AND EVALUATION REPORT

There are many data analysis tools available to evaluators. Although this falls within the purview and expertise of data analysts and data scientists, as an evaluator, it is and becomes advantageous to be conversant and knowledgeable to a large extent in these fields, as well.

Data analysis tools are software and programs that collect and analyse data to improve processes and help uncover insights to make data-driven decisions.

Types Of Data Analysis: The four types of data analysis are:
- ✓ Descriptive Analysis.
- ✓ Diagnostic Analysis.
- ✓ Predictive Analysis.
- ✓ Prescriptive Analysis.

Descriptive Analysis: The first type of data analysis is descriptive analysis. It is at the foundation of all data insight. It is the simplest and most commonly used form of data in business today. Descriptive analysis answers the "what happened" by summarising past data, usually in the form of dashboards.

The biggest use of descriptive analysis in business is to track Key Performance Indicators (KPIS). KPIS describe how a business is performing based on chosen benchmarks.

Applications of descriptive analysis include:
- ✓ KPI dashboards.
- ✓ Monthly revenue reports.
- ✓ Sales lead overview.

After asking the main question of "what happened", the next step is to dive deeper and ask why it happened. This leads us to the next data analysis type.

Diagnostic Analysis takes the insights found from descriptive analytics and drills down to find the causes of those outcomes. Organisations make use of this type of analytics as it creates more connections between data and identifies patterns of behaviour.

A critical aspect of diagnostic analysis is creating detailed information. When new problems arise, you may have already collected certain data about the issue. By already having the data at your disposal, it ends up having to repeat work and makes all problems interconnected.

Applications of diagnostic analysis include:

- ✓ A logistics company investigating the cause of slow shipments within and to certain regions and/or localities.
- ✓ A fast-food company is drilling down to determine which marketing activities increased sales.

Predictive Analysis: Predictive analysis attempts to answer the question, "What is likely to happen?" This type of analytics utilises previous data to make predictions about future outcomes.

This type of analysis is another step up from the descriptive and diagnostic analyses. Predictive analysis uses the data we have summarised to make logical predictions of the outcomes of events. This analysis relies on statistical modelling, which requires additional technology and manpower to forecast. It is also important to understand that forecasting is only an estimate; the accuracy of predictions relies on the quality and detail of the data.

While descriptive and diagnostic analysis are common business practices, predictive analysis is where many organisations begin to show signs of difficulty. Some organisations do not have the manpower to implement predictive analysis in the areas of business they desire. Others are not yet willing to invest in analysis teams across every department or are not prepared to educate current teams.

Applications of predictive analysis include:

- ✓ Risk Assessment.
- ✓ Sales Forecasting.
- ✓ Using customer segmentation to determine which leads have the best chance of converting.

Prescriptive Analysis: The final type of data analysis is the most sought-after, but few organisations are truly equipped to perform it. A prescriptive analysis is the frontier of data analysis, combining the insight from all previous analyses to determine the course of action to take in a current problem or decision.

Prescriptive analysis utilises state-of-the-art technology and data practices. It is a huge organisational commitment, and companies must be sure that they are ready and willing to put forth the effort and resources.

Artificial Intelligence (AI) is a perfect example of prescriptive analytics. AI systems consume a large amount of data to continuously learn and use this information to make informed decisions. Well-designed AI systems are capable of communicating these decisions and even putting those decisions into action. Business processes can be performed and optimised daily without a human doing anything with artificial intelligence.

Currently, most of the big data-driven companies (Google, Apple, Facebook, Netflix, etc.) are utilising prescriptive analytics and AI to improve decision-making. For other organisations, the jump to predictive and prescriptive analytics can be daunting, but not insurmountable. As technology continues to improve and more professionals are educated in data, we will see more companies entering the data-driven realm.

Each of these types of data analysis is connected and relies on the others to a certain degree. They each serve a different purpose and provide varying insights. Moving from descriptive analysis towards predictive and prescriptive analysis requires much more technical ability but also unlocks more insight for your organisation.

Data Analysis Tools: There are various data analysis tools available to data analysts that evaluators can make use of. From personal experience, I am of the view that tools with good visualisation packages and capabilities are more/most suitable for evaluation and evaluators. Such as suitable tools/applications are:

- ✓ Microsoft Excel
- ✓ Power BI,
- ✓ Tableau,

- ✓ SPSS (Statistical Packages for Social Scientists),
- ✓ Etc.

Development Of An Evaluation Report

Your findings/analysis needs to be effectively communicated to the right and appropriate sources/channels (recipients). Hence, you need to ask yourself, is my report "SMART"? SMART is an acronym for these five (5) attributes:

- ✓ S – Specific,
- ✓ M – Measurable,
- ✓ A – Accurate,
- ✓ R – Reasonable/Reliable,
- ✓ T – Time-bound.

Reporting: Although your report MUST be based on scientific/facts (and not subjective), you need to keep the following in mind:

- ✓ Am I in line with the project objective(s)?
- ✓ Am I in consonance with other stakeholders?
  - ➢ Do I understand others' needs?
  - ➢ Will my findings' communication serve a communal/joint purpose?
  - ➢ Are my data and findings reliable?

Activities

- ✓ Create a report on the boy/girl ratio in Science Subjects for JSS between 2007 – 2010.
- ✓ Create a report on the boy/girl ratio in English Language and Mathematics for JSS between 2007 – 2010.
- ✓ Create a report based on 1 & 2 above for your regional coordinator.

NB: You can come up with your figures that you can easily work with as practice.

CHAPTER TWELVE (12) – USES OF RESULTS

USES OF MONITORING AND EVALUATION RESULTS

This handbook is all about Monitoring and Evaluation in its entirety, and one naturally would have seen without even deliberately focusing on it, that is, the benefits and usefulness of an evaluation, to which this chapter is dedicated, and in some more specific details.

Monitoring and Evaluation exercises are critical for understanding the effectiveness of any project or programme. Regular assessment allows you to identify successes and areas where improvements can be made. It also ensures accountability, allowing stakeholders to track progress and hold each other responsible for achieving goals.

Monitoring and Evaluation also provide information for decision-making and decision-makers, helping to ensure that policies and programmes are based on evidence rather than guesswork – decisions are not emotive, but rather scientific and analytic. Furthermore, they are essential for accountability, as they provide information on how public funds are being used and what results are achieved.

The use of Monitoring and Evaluation results is not limited to our regular projects and programmes; they are also useful, for example, in monitoring and evaluating **good governance**, which is essential for any organisation and any economy to succeed and thrive. But how do you know if you/we are succeeding as organisations, individuals, projects/programmes and/or even as a nation?

Monitoring and Evaluation are key components of good governance. They provide the data and evidence you need to make informed decisions, track the progress of various agencies, arms of government/governance, and organisations, and ensure accountability.

With good and well-defined, and identified indicators, Monitoring and Evaluation are essential for good governance as they provide feedback on the effectiveness of policies, programmes, projects, and services. They allow governments to identify successes and areas for improvement, enabling them to adjust their strategies and ensure that scarce resources are used judiciously and most effectively.

Performance Measurement: Valuable exercise not the least, because it provides an opportunity and a framework for asking fundamental questions such as:

- ✓ What are you trying to achieve?
- ✓ What does "success" look like?
- ✓ How will you know if or when you have achieved it (success)?

The following are four (4) issues central to how we evaluate our performance:

- ✓ Well-defined objectives – so we know what we are trying to achieve.
- ✓ A clear strategy – explaining how we propose to get there.
- ✓ Monitorable indicators – to know if we are on track.
- ✓ Evaluation of results – for both accountability and learning.

Monitoring and Evaluation can help to ensure that public services are delivered cost-effectively and equitably, allowing governments to identify and address any disparities in access to the services dedicated to the local and state communities, and even at the national level.

The Importance Of Evaluation In Achieving Organisational Goals

Evaluation helps organisations measure progress towards their goals and objectives, as well as identify areas of strength and weakness. This is an essential part of the decision-making process and can provide invaluable insight into where improvements need to be made and what successes need to be recognised and celebrated. Evaluation is a critical tool for assessing performance and determining the effectiveness of strategies, processes, systems, and products.

Through the evaluation process, organisations can gain objective data to inform their decisions, help set goals, and track progress. In addition, it provides a means of assessing overall performance to make meaningful changes that can positively influence outcomes. Ultimately, evaluation can play a pivotal role in driving organisational growth and success.

It also serves as a means of assessing the effectiveness of strategies and initiatives, ensuring that resources are being used in the most effective way possible. Evaluation helps to identify which aspects of a project are most important to the overall success, and which elements should be prioritised. It serves as a tool for measuring progress, helping to ensure that objectives are being met and that resources are being used wisely.

Additionally, evaluation provides insight into where changes can be made to improve performance and increase efficiency. Through the use of the importance of evaluation, organisations can ensure that they are making the best use of their resources to achieve their desired results.

Regular evaluation can be used to adjust course and redirect efforts to achieve desired outcomes, making it an indispensable tool for any successful organisation. Also, evaluation is an incredibly important tool for organisations to ensure that their efforts lead to desirable outcomes.

Evaluation allows organisations to identify what is working and identify and analyse areas of improvement, so that resources can be allocated accordingly, and goals can be reached more efficiently. Evaluation is, therefore, an indispensable factor for any successful organisation.

Monitoring and Evaluation is an essential tool for any organisation that wants to ensure its objectives are being achieved efficiently and effectively. By investing in Monitoring and Evaluation systems and processes, organisations can ensure that their activities are being monitored and evaluated, which will help them to make strategic decisions and optimise resources.

In addition to these benefits, Monitoring and Evaluation also provides organisations with valuable insights into the impact of their interventions and the strengths and weaknesses of their operations. Ultimately, it is essential for long-term organisational success.

In summary,

- ✓ Monitoring and Evaluation are important tools that can help organisations measure their progress and assess the effectiveness of the strategies they have implemented.
- ✓ Tracking results over time can provide insight into where there is room for improvement, allowing organisations to adjust their strategies accordingly.
- ✓ Monitoring and Evaluation are also essential when it comes to securing funding and demonstrating impact to external stakeholders.

- ✓ Monitoring and Evaluation are critical for understanding the effectiveness of any project and programme.
- ✓ Regular assessment allows you to identify successes and areas where improvements can be made.
- ✓ It also ensures accountability, allowing stakeholders to track progress and hold each other responsible for achieving goals.
- ✓ Monitoring and Evaluation can help identify areas where improvement is needed and track progress over time.
- ✓ It also allows for better decision-making by providing data-driven insights into what is working and what is not working.
- ✓ Regular Monitoring and Evaluation can also help ensure that resources are allocated effectively and goals are being met.

Uses Of Monitoring and Evaluation Include:

- ✓ The efficiency and effectiveness of public expenditure.
- ✓ Cut expenses.
- ✓ Prioritise programmes, projects, and activities.
- ✓ Identify what has worked/is working.
- ✓ What is not working or what has not worked?
- ✓ How do we improve the use(s) of resources?
- ✓ Involve all stakeholders (show their importance)

Where Programme Monitoring And Evaluation Is Helpful

Frequent Reasons:

- ✓ Understand, verify, or increase the impact of products or services on customers or clients. These "outcomes" evaluations are increasingly required by non-profit funders as verification that the non-profits are indeed helping their constituents.
- ✓ Improve delivery mechanisms to be more efficient and less costly. Over time, product or service delivery ends up being an inefficient collection of activities that are less efficient and more costly than needed. Monitoring and Evaluation can identify programme strengths and weaknesses and help improve the programme.

✓ Verify that you are doing what you think you are doing – Monitoring and Evaluation can verify if the programme is running as originally planned and intended.

Other Reasons:
- ✓ Facilitate management's thinking about what their programme is all about, including its goals, and how it meets its goals.
- ✓ Produce data or verified results that can be used for public relations and promoting services in the community.
- ✓ Produce valid comparisons between programmes to decide which should be retained, for example, budget cuts.
- ✓ Fully examine and describe effective programmes for duplication elsewhere.

Evidence-Based Policy Making: A policy process that helps planners make better-informed decisions by putting the best available evidence at the centre of the policy process.

Evidence may include information produced by integrated Monitoring and Evaluation systems, academic research, historical experience, and "good practice" information.

In contrast to an opinion-based policy which relies heavily on either the selective use of evidence or on the untested views of individuals or groups often inspired by ideological standpoints, prejudices, or speculative conjecture. Many organisations are moving from "opinion-based policy" towards "evidence-based policy" and "evidence-influenced policy".

Making Effective Use of Evidence

Improving the "understandability" of evidence - translate evidence into a language that is useful to the users of evidence.
- ✓ Effective dissemination and wide access.
- ✓ Incentives to use evidence: Practitioners need incentives to do effective things.

Benchmarking the Educational System for Results

A case study:

Education Systems: Two Broad Categories

✓ System performance: Student performance in national and international assessments.

✓ System health: Policies and other factors determining the performance. For example, equal educational opportunities, teacher quality programmes, reducing barriers to learning, curricula, students' examination and assessment.

These can be done by:

Evaluating the impact of specific interventions:

✓ Class size reductions.

✓ School-based management.

✓ Additional teachers.

✓ Policy reforms (for example, extension of compulsory schooling, vocational education, public-private partnerships) on student learning.

✓ Continual updating of the monitoring system; student, school, and system variables since the interactions among them jointly produce student learning.

Important Criteria

Assessment systems: Increasingly recognised as important for student assessment in improving education quality and student learning depends on three sets of factors.

1. The overall enabling environment for assessment activity:

✓ Assessment policies.

✓ Organisational structures.

✓ Human/fiscal resources.

2. The degree to which assessment activity is integrated with the rest of the education system (that is, the degree of alignment with content and performance standards, curricula, textbooks, and teacher training).

3. The technical quality of the instruments used (that is, psychometric validity and reliability, Clarke 2009).

✓ Secondary school tracking: Education plays a central role in preparing individuals to enter the labour force, as well as equipping them with the skills to engage in lifelong learning experiences.

Technical and vocational education and training (TVET): considered to be a key supplier of a skilled workforce for countries at all stages of development.

Regulatory framework for private and public education: Public-private partnerships (PPPs), a policy alternative that allows governments to establish linkages between governance and service delivery by conditioning public funding to performance indicators while building capacity and allowing flexibility to operators to meet a variety of student needs.

- ✓ School-level decision-making, autonomy, and accountability (school-based management, SMB).
- ✓ Decentralising decision-making encourages demand and ensures that schools reflect local priorities and values.
- ✓ School-based management (SBM): a way to decentralise decision-making power in education.

SBM emphasises:

- ✓ The individual school (as represented by any combination of principals, teachers, parents, students, and other members of the school community) is the primary unit for improving education.
- ✓ The redistribution of decision-making authority over school operations is the primary means by which this improvement can be stimulated and sustained.

SBM can improve schooling outcomes (Barrera, Fasih, and Patrinos 2009)

- ✓ SBM policies changed the dynamics of the school, either because parents got more involved or because teachers' actions changed.
- ✓ Several studies show that SBM had a positive impact on repetition rates, failure rates, and, to a lesser degree, dropout rates.
- ✓ Teacher policies.
- ✓ Access to quality education for all children depends on recruiting skilled and motivated teachers.
- ✓ Determine how much each student learns.

NB: Teacher policies are one among the several system-wide factors that directly influence the delivery of education and help students develop cognitive and non-cognitive skills.

After Monitoring And Evaluation, What Next?

Monitoring and Evaluation have little value if the organisation or project does not act on the information that comes out of the analysis of the data collected. Once you have the findings, conclusions, and recommendations from your Monitoring and Evaluation process, you need to:

✓ Report to your stakeholders.

✓ Learn from the overall process.

✓ Make effective decisions about how to move forward, and, if necessary,

✓ Deal with resistance to the necessary changes within the organisation or project, or even among other stakeholders.

Action Plan

✓ An action plan agreed by relevant stakeholders should include information on specific outputs expected and activities that will be carried out during the Monitoring and Evaluation Plan's life span (or shorter), with details including the responsible unit, budget, and timing.

✓ This can be developed with the support of the Monitoring and Evaluation System Strengthening Tool and should be considered a living document, constantly monitored, reviewed, and updated annually.

✓ To be sure, we must continue to evaluate. Evaluation contributes to three basic functions:

1. Accountability: making sure that public institutions and their staff are held accountable for their performance.

2. Allocation: making sure that resources are allocated to those activities that contribute most effectively to achieving the basic objectives of the institution.

3. Learning: making sure we learn from our successes and failures, to do things better in the future.

- ✓ The major issues of evaluation are management rather than methodological ones; they are about how and where evaluation should be organised, located, planned, and managed to best affect decision-making. They are about managing for performance, rather than simply measuring performance.
- ✓ A major part of this aim is creating the right incentives for evaluation on both the supply and demand sides.
- ✓ However, the issue of incentives, demand, and supply calls into question the purposes of evaluation. Depending on how evaluation information is to be used, incentives may operate differently.
- ✓ Increasingly, the evaluation literature stresses evaluation as part of continuous learning for performance improvement, improving management's knowledge base. Evaluation is thus seen as a normal and valued part of the management cycle.

GLOSSARY

MONITORING AND EVALUATION TERMS

This glossary includes terms typically used in the area of Monitoring and Evaluation (M&E) and provides the basis for facilitating a common understanding of M&E., most terms in the glossary can be used generically.

Accountability: responsibility for the use of resources and the decisions made, as well as the obligation to demonstrate that work has been done in compliance with agreed-upon rules and standards and to report fairly and accurately on performance results vis-a-vis mandated roles and/or plans.

Activity: actions taken or work performed through which inputs such as funds, technical assistance, and other types of resources are mobilised to produce specific outputs.

Assumptions: hypotheses about factors or risks that could affect the progress or success of an intervention. Intervention results depend on whether or not the assumptions made prove to be correct.

Attribution: the ascription of a causal link between observed changes and a specific intervention.

Audit: an independent, objective quality assurance activity designed to add value and improve an organisation's operations. It helps an organisation accomplish its objectives by bringing a systematic, disciplined approach to assess and improve the effectiveness of risk management, control, and governance processes.

Note: Internal auditing is conducted by a unit reporting to management, while external auditing is conducted by an independent organisation.

Baseline: the status of services and outcome-related measures such as knowledge, attitudes, norms, behaviours, and conditions before an intervention, against which progress can be assessed or comparisons made.

Benchmark: a reference point or standard against which performance or achievements can be assessed.

Note: A benchmark refers to the performance that has been achieved in the recent past by other comparable organisations, or what can be reasonably inferred to have been achieved in similar circumstances.

Beneficiaries: the individuals, groups, or organisations, whether targeted or not, that benefit directly or indirectly from the intervention.

Case Study: a methodological approach that describes a situation, individual, or the like and that typically incorporates data-gathering activities (for example, interviews, observations, questionnaires) at selected sites or programs/projects. Case studies are characterised by purposive selection of sites or small samples; the expectation of generalizability is less than that in many other forms of research. The findings are used to report to stakeholders, make recommendations for program/project improvement, and share lessons learned.

Conclusions: point out the factors of success and failure of the evaluated intervention, with special attention paid to the intended and unintended results, and more generally to any other strength or weakness. A conclusion draws on data collection and analysis undertaken through a transparent chain of arguments.

Coverage: the extent to which a program/intervention is being implemented in the right places (geographic coverage) and is reaching its intended target population (individual coverage).

Data: specific quantitative and qualitative information or facts that are collected and analysed.

Economic Evaluation: use applied analytical techniques to identify, measure, value, and compare the costs and outcomes of alternative interventions. Types of economic evaluations include cost-benefit, cost-effectiveness, and cost-efficiency evaluations.

Effectiveness: the extent to which a program/intervention has achieved its objectives under normal conditions in a real-life setting.

Efficacy: the extent to which an intervention produces the expected results under ideal conditions in a controlled environment.

Efficiency: a measure of how economic inputs (resources such as funds, expertise, and time) are converted into results.

Evaluation: the rigorous, scientifically based collection of information about program/intervention activities, characteristics, and outcomes that determine the merit or worth of the program/intervention. Evaluation studies provide credible information for use in improving programs/interventions, identifying lessons learned, and informing decisions about future resource allocation.

Formative Evaluation: a type of evaluation intended to improve the performance of a program or intervention. A formative evaluation is usually undertaken during the design and pre-testing of the intervention or program, but it can also be conducted early in the implementation phase, particularly if implementation activities are not going as expected.

Goal: a broad statement of a desired, usually longer-term, outcome of a program/intervention. Goals express general program/intervention intentions and help guide the development of a program/intervention. Each goal has a set of related, specific objectives that, if met, will collectively permit the achievement of the stated goal.

Impact: the long-term, cumulative effect of programs/interventions over a period on what they ultimately aim to change, such as a change in HIV infection, AIDS-related morbidity, and mortality.

Note: Impacts at a population level are rarely attributable to a single program/intervention, but a specific program/intervention may, together with other programs/interventions, contribute to impacts on a population.

Impact Evaluation: a type of evaluation that assesses the rise and fall of impacts, such as disease prevalence and incidence, as a function of HIV programs/interventions. Impacts on a population seldom can be attributed to a single program/intervention; therefore, an evaluation of impacts on a population generally entails a rigorous design that assesses the combined effects of several programs/interventions for at-risk populations.

Impact Monitoring: tracking of health-related events, such as the prevalence or incidence of a particular disease; in the field of public health, impact monitoring is usually referred to as "surveillance".

Incidence: the number of new cases of a disease that occur in a specified population during a specified period.

Indicator: a quantitative or qualitative variable that provides a valid and reliable way to measure achievement, assess performance, or reflect changes connected to an intervention.

Note: Single indicators are limited in their utility for understanding program effects (that is, what is working or is not working, and why?). Indicator data should be collected and interpreted as part of a set of indicators. Indicator sets alone cannot determine the effectiveness of a program or collection of programs; for this, good evaluation designs are necessary.

Inputs: the financial, human, and material resources used in a program/intervention.

Internal Evaluation: an evaluation of an intervention conducted by a unit and/or individuals who report to the management of the organisation responsible for the financial support, design, and/or implementation of the intervention.

Intervention: a specific activity or set of activities intended to bring about change in some aspect(s) of the status of the target population (for example, HIV risk reduction, improving the quality-of-service delivery).

Lessons Learned: generalisations based on evaluation experiences with programs, interventions, or policies that abstract from the specific circumstances to broader situations. Frequently, lessons highlight strengths or weaknesses in preparation, design, and implementation that affect performance, outcome, and impact.

Logical Framework: a management tool used to improve the design of interventions. It involves identifying strategic elements (inputs, outputs, activities, outcomes, impact) and their causal relationships, indicators, and the assumptions of risks that may influence success and failure. It thus facilitates the planning, execution, monitoring, and evaluation of an intervention.

Meta-Evaluation: a type of evaluation designed to aggregate findings from a series of evaluations. It can also be used to denote the evaluation of an evaluation to judge its quality and/or assess the performance of the evaluators.

Monitoring: routine tracking and reporting of priority information about a programme/ project, its inputs and intended outputs, outcomes, and impacts.

Monitoring and Evaluation Plan: a multi-year implementation strategy for the collection, analysis, and use of data needed for program/project management and accountability purposes. The plan describes the data needs to be linked to a specific program/project; the M&E activities that need to be undertaken to satisfy the data needs and the specific data collection procedures and tools; the standardised indicators that need to be collected for routine monitoring and regular reporting; the components of the M&E system that need to be implemented and the roles and responsibilities of different organisations/individuals in their implementation.

Implementation: how data will be used for program/project management and accountability purposes. The plan indicates resource requirement estimates and outlines a strategy for resource mobilisation.

Monitoring and Evaluation Workplan: an annual costed M&E plan that describes the priority M&E activities for the year and the roles and responsibilities of organisations/individuals for their implementation; the cost of each activity and the funding identified; a timeline for delivery of all products/outputs. The work plan is used for coordinating M&E activities and assessing the progress of M&E implementation throughout the year. Note: A national HIV M&E work plan is an annual plan that is developed with the participation of those stakeholders who have roles and responsibilities for the M&E activities identified in the work plan.

Objective: a statement of a desired program/intervention result that meets the criteria of being Specific, Measurable, Achievable, Realistic, and Time-bound (SMART).

Operational Research: systematic and objective assessment of the availability, accessibility, quality, and/or sustainability of services designed to improve service delivery. It assesses only factors that are under the control of program/project managers, such as improving the quality of services, increasing training and supervision of staff members, and adding new service components.

Outcome: short-term and medium-term effects of an intervention's outputs, such as a change in knowledge, attitudes, beliefs, and behaviours.

Outcome Evaluation: a type of evaluation that determines if, and by how much, intervention activities or services achieved their intended outcomes. An outcome evaluation attempts to attribute observed changes to the intervention tested.

Note: An outcome evaluation is methodologically rigorous and generally requires a comparative element in its design, such as a control or comparison group, although it is possible to use statistical techniques in some instances when control/comparison groups are not available (e.g., for the evaluation of a national program).

Outcome Monitoring: tracking of variables that have been adopted as valid and reliable measures (that is, indicators) of the desired program/intervention outcomes. Outcome monitoring does not infer causality; changes in outcomes may be attributable to multiple factors, not just a specified program/intervention.

Note: With national AIDS programs, outcome monitoring is typically conducted through population-based surveys (i.e., representative of the target population, not necessarily the general population).

Outputs: the results of program/intervention activities; the direct products or deliverables of program/intervention activities, such as the number of HIV counselling sessions completed, the number of people served, and the number of condoms distributed.

Performance: the degree to which an intervention or organisation operates according to specific criteria/standards/guidelines or achieves results following stated goals or plans.

Process Evaluation: a type of evaluation that focuses on program/intervention implementation, including, but not limited to, access to services, whether services reach the intended population, how services are delivered, client satisfaction and perceptions about needs and services, and management practices. In addition, a process evaluation might provide an understanding of cultural, sociopolitical, legal, and economic contexts that affect the implementation of the program/intervention.

Programme: an overarching national or sub-national response to a disease. A program generally includes a set of interventions marshalled to attain specific global, regional, country, or subnational objectives; and involves multiple activities that may cut across sectors, themes, and/or geographic areas.

Programme Evaluation: a study that intends to control a health problem or improve a public health program or service. The intended benefits of the program are primarily or exclusively for the study participants or the study participants' community (i.e., the population from which the study participants were sampled); data collected are needed to assess and/or improve the program or service, and/or the health of the study participants or the study participants' community. The knowledge that is generated does not typically extend beyond the population or program from which the data are collected.

Project: an intervention designed to achieve specific objectives within specified resources and implementation schedules, often within the framework of a broader program.

Qualitative Data: data collected using qualitative methods, such as interviews, focus groups, observation, and key informant interviews. Qualitative data can provide an understanding of social situations and interactions, as well as people's values, perceptions, motivations, and reactions. Qualitative data are generally expressed in narrative form, pictures or objects (i.e., not numerically). Note: A qualitative study aims to provide a complete, detailed description.

Quality Assurance: planned and systematic processes concerned with assessing and improving the merit or worth of an intervention or its compliance with given standards.

Note: Examples of quality assurance activities include appraisal, results-based management reviews, and evaluations.

Quantitative Data: data collected using quantitative methods, such as surveys. Quantitative data are measured on a numerical scale, can be analysed using statistical methods, and can be displayed using tables, charts, histograms, and graphs.

Note: A quantitative study aims to classify features, count them, and construct statistical models in an attempt to explain what is observed.

Relevance: the extent to which the objectives, outputs, or outcomes of an intervention are consistent with beneficiaries' requirements, organisations' policies, country needs, and/or global priorities.

Reliability: consistency or dependability of data collected through the repeated use of a scientific instrument, or a data collection procedure used under the same conditions.

Research: a study that intends to generate or contribute to generalizable knowledge to improve public health practice, that is, the study intends to generate new information that has relevance beyond the population or program from which data are collected. Research typically attempts to make statements about how the different variables under study, in controlled circumstances, affect one another at a given point in time.

Results: the outputs, outcomes, or impacts (intended or unintended, positive and/or negative) of an intervention.

Results-Based Management (RBM): a management strategy focusing on performance and achievement of outputs, outcomes, and impacts.

Stakeholder: a person, group, or entity who has a direct or indirect role and interest in the goals or objectives and implementation of a program/intervention and/or its evaluation.

Summative Evaluation: a type of evaluation conducted at the end of an intervention (or a phase of that intervention) to determine the extent to which anticipated outcomes were produced. It is designed to provide information about the merit or worth of the intervention.

Sustainability (of a program): the likelihood that political and financial support will last to maintain the program.

Target: the objective a program/intervention is working towards, expressed as a measurable value; the desired value for an indicator at a particular point in time.

Target group: a specific group of people who are to benefit from the result of the intervention.

Terms of Reference (TOR): written document presenting the purpose and scope of the evaluation, the methods to be used, the standards against which performance is to be assessed or analyses to be conducted, the resources and time allocated, and the reporting requirements.

Validity: the extent to which a measurement or test accurately measures what is intended to be measured.

Value Judgment: is a judgment of the rightness or wrongness of an input to a project, programme or intervention, or the usefulness of it, based on a comparison or other relativity. As a generalisation, a value judgment can refer to a judgment based upon a particular set of values or on a particular value system, usually based on the outputs and outcomes.

Sources:
> Evaluation Working Group of the UNAIDS Monitoring and Evaluation Reference
> Group (MERG) (2008). Glossary of M&E Terms. Geneva, Switzerland: MERG Evaluation Technical Working Group, 2007.
> Global AIDS Program (GAP) (2003). Monitoring & Evaluation Capacity Building for Program Improvement. Field Guide. Atlanta, USA: GAP, Centres for Disease Control and Prevention.
> Joint United Nations Programme on HIV/AIDS (UNAIDS) (2007). A framework for monitoring and evaluating HIV prevention programmes for most at-risk populations. Geneva, Switzerland: UNAIDS.
> Organisation for Economic Co-operation and Development (OECD) (2002). Glossary of key terms in evaluation and result-based management. Paris, France: OECD.

➤ Rugg, D., Peersman, G., & Carael, M. (Eds.) (2004). Global advances in HIV/AIDS monitoring and evaluation. New Directions for Evaluation, 2004 (103).

REFERENCES

- https://insight7.io/top-7-data-collection-tools-in-monitoring-and-evaluation/
- https://resourcecentre.savethechildren.net/document/toolkit-monitoring-and-evaluating-childrens-participation-tools-monitoring-and-evaluating/
- https://www.sopact.com/guides/monitoring-and-evaluation-tools
- https://tools4dev.org/blog/books-in-monitoring-and-evaluation/
- https://tools4dev.org/resources/how-to-write-a-monitoring-and-evaluation-framework/
- https://www.amazon.com/Mastering-Art-Monitoring-Evaluation-Beginners/dp/B0BSJPYVC6
- https://www.betterevaluation.org/sites/default/files/pme-handbook.pdf
- https://tools4dev.org/resources/me-framework-template/
- https://tools4dev.org/elearning/how-to-write-an-me-framework/
- https://tools4dev.org/resources/monitoring-evaluation-plan-template/
- https://www.measureevaluation.org/resources/training/capacity-building-resources/basic-me-concepts-portuguese/IFRC_Monitoring%20and%20Evaluation%20handbook.pdf
- https://www.crc.uri.edu/download/Phil_Guide_lowres_web.pdf
- https://www.therobertsontrust.org.uk/media/ppjiqbue/trt_monitoring_and_evaluation_tools_and_techniques.pdf
- https://insight7.io/top-7-data-collection-tools-in-monitoring-and-evaluation/